continued . . .

"*Charlotte au Chocolat* is simply exquisite. Savor it. Devour it. Silver has taken a cool-eyed, unsentimental look at her unique and strange childhood and made lavish, glorious art of it."

—Lily King,
author of *Father of the Rain*

"Charlotte Silver has written a love song to a remarkable restaurant and a vanished world. I devoured these pages with the same enthusiasm as the author brings to pheasant's legs and steak tartare on toast."

—Margot Livesey,
author of *Eva Moves the Furniture*

"Reading *Charlotte au Chocolat* is like sitting down to a sumptuous, many-coursed dinner—and then, after taking your last bite of Queen Mother's cake, having the pleasure of lingering in the kitchen, where a cast of vivid characters conjures culinary magic until closing time. A feast of a book!"

—Allison Hoover Bartlett,
author of *The Man Who Loved Books Too Much*

CHARLOTTE *au* CHOCOLAT

MEMORIES OF

A RESTAURANT GIRLHOOD

Charlotte Silver

RIVERHEAD BOOKS

New York

RIVERHEAD BOOKS
Published by the Penguin Group
Penguin Group (USA) Inc.
375 Hudson Street, New York, New York 10014, USA

Penguin Group (Canada), 90 Eglinton Avenue East, Suite 700, Toronto, Ontario M4P 2Y3, Canada
(a division of Pearson Penguin Canada Inc.) • Penguin Books Ltd., 80 Strand, London WC2R 0RL,
England • Penguin Group Ireland, 25 St. Stephen's Green, Dublin 2, Ireland (a division of Penguin
Books Ltd.) • Penguin Group (Australia), 250 Camberwell Road, Camberwell, Victoria 3124, Australia
(a division of Pearson Australia Group Pty. Ltd.) • Penguin Books India Pvt. Ltd., 11 Community
Centre, Panchsheel Park, New Delhi—110 017, India • Penguin Group (NZ), 67 Apollo Drive,
Rosedale, Auckland 0632, New Zealand (a division of Pearson New Zealand Ltd.) • Penguin Books
(South Africa) (Pty.) Ltd., 24 Sturdee Avenue, Rosebank, Johannesburg 2196, South Africa

Penguin Books Ltd., Registered Offices: 80 Strand, London WC2R 0RL, England

While the author has made every effort to provide accurate telephone numbers,
Internet addresses, and other contact information at the time of publication, neither the publisher
nor the author assumes any responsibility for errors, or for changes that occur after publication.
Further, the publisher does not have any control over and does not assume any
responsibility for author or third-party websites or their content.

First Riverhead hardcover edition: February 2012
First Riverhead trade paperback edition: February 2013
Riverhead trade paperback ISBN: 978-1-59448-650-0

The Library of Congress has catalogued the Riverhead hardcover edition as follows:

Silver, Charlotte.
Charlotte au chocolat : memories of a restaurant girlhood / Charlotte Silver.
p.   cm.
ISBN 978-1-59448-815-3
1. Upstairs at the Pudding (Cambridge, Mass.).   2. Silver, Charlotte.   3. Cambridge (Mass.)—
Social life and customs.   I. Title.
TX945.5.U67S55   2012   2011046847
647.95744'4—dc23

PRINTED IN THE UNITED STATES OF AMERICA

10   9   8   7   6   5   4   3   2   1

Penguin is committed to publishing works of quality and integrity.
In that spirit, we are proud to offer this book to our readers;
however, the story, the experiences, and the words
are the author's alone.

ALWAYS LEARNING   PEARSON

For my mother and M. C. D.

CONTENTS

PROLOGUE

I grew up rich. The setting—or stage set—of my childhood was the velvety pink-and-green dining room of my mother's restaurant, Upstairs at the Pudding, located above the Hasty Pudding Club in a redbrick Victorian building at 10 Holyoke Street in Harvard Square. My life was not a child's life of jungle gyms and Velcro sneakers, but of soft lighting, stiff petticoats, rolling pins smothered in flour, and candied violets in wax paper. It was a life of manners, of air kisses, of "How do you dos," and a life for which I needed six party dresses a year, three every spring and three every winter. We were rich. Everybody knew it.

Yet we were not; we were not rich at all. For as long as I could remember, the restaurant had tottered on the brink of collapse. I always knew we would lose it one day. And we did lose it; we did.

In my memories of my childhood, it is always the nighttime and never the day, and I am always waiting. Waiting for
what? I am waiting for one season to end and another to
begin and for the menus to change—for soft-boiled eggs
and fiddlehead ferns in spring; for lobster claws cracked
open and bathed in hot lashes of nasturtium butter in summer; for baked apples in thickened pools of heavy cream in
fall; and finally for winter, season of prime rib and potatoes
gratin, caviar and sweetbreads, and chocolate, chocolate,
chocolate. I am waiting for a waiter to bring me one Shirley
Temple, and then another. I am waiting for this waiter to
leave, as I know he will someday, and for another to take his
place. I am waiting for my mother to brush past me in a haze
of Joy perfume and plant a Coco Pink kiss on my cheek. I
am waiting for my father who left us to return. I am waiting
to go home at the end of the night.

I am waiting to grow up and, one day, leave this world.

One

HASTY PUDDING

$\mathcal{M}$y name is Charlotte, and I was named for the dessert charlotte au chocolat, which used to be the signature dessert of the restaurant.

When I was a child, charlottes—French desserts made traditionally out of brioche, ladyfingers, or sponge and baked in a charlotte mold—were everywhere. Charlotte au chocolat wasn't the only variety, though being chocolate, it had the edge on my mother's autumn-season apple charlotte braised with brioche and poached in clarified butter, and even on the magnificent charlotte Malakoff she used to serve in the summer: raspberries, slivered almonds, and Grand Marnier in valleys of vanilla custard.

But it is charlotte au chocolat, being my namesake dessert, that I remember most, for we offered it on the menu all year long. I walked into the pastry station and saw them cooling in their rusted tin molds on the counter. I saw them scooped onto lace doilies and smothered in Chantilly cream, starred with candied violets and sprigs of wet mint. I saw them lit by birthday candles. I saw them arranged, by the dozens, on silver trays for private parties. I saw them on customers' plates, destroyed, the Chantilly cream like a tumbled snowbank streaked with soot from the chocolate. And charlottes smelled delightful: they smelled richer, I thought, than any dessert in the world. The smell made me think of black velvet holiday dresses and grown-up perfumes in crystal flasks. It made me want to collapse and never eat again.

I was also scared of charlottes, scared that someday I might become one. One of the line cooks once said to me, "One of these nights when we run out of charlottes, we're going to plop you on a plate and top you in whipped cream. Oh, the customers won't mind. I hear that little girls taste yummy."

I believed him. I even believed that I would fit on a plate. In those days, I seemed that small, and the rest of the world that big.

My parents first laid eyes on the dining room of the Hasty Pudding Club when my mother was pregnant with me. Their good friend and future business partner Mary-Catherine Deibel was with them, too, that day. The

three of them were shocked to discover that the undergraduates had trashed the beautiful old-world room with the
hunter green walls and the domed, forty-foot ceilings that
were majestic even by Harvard standards. Cleaning it up
before opening for business, not long after I was born, they
uncovered soiled toothpicks, bow ties, and garters. A hardened creamy pink substance—my father said it must have
come from strawberry daiquiris—crusted the green velvet
carpet that always smelled, even after being vacuumed, of a
vague Ivy League potpourri of brandy and mothballs and
after-dinner cigars.

The Hasty Pudding Club, founded in 1770, is the oldest
student society at Harvard. In 1982 when my parents opened
their restaurant, which they named Upstairs at the Pudding,
the Club still owned the building at 10 Holyoke Street, right
across from the gates of Harvard Yard. But they already were
having financial problems, a sign of things to come. They
agreed to rent space to a tenant because they needed the
income, and converting the top floor of the building into a
fine restaurant was a genteel solution to their financial woes.

The restaurant, then, was that rare place where the exclu-
sive Harvard "final clubs" and the public met. The magnificent space still retained the private air of a club, but the door
to the building was open to all; anybody could walk upstairs
and dine there. From the beginning, the restaurant was a

favorite with Harvard professors and presidents. It was the kind of restaurant where undergraduates, used to eating at The Tasty and Pinocchio's, could count on their parents taking them for steak dinners. It did a fabulous business for Harvard—as well as MIT—graduation. Boston was still a baked-beans-and-broiled-scrod kind of town then, and fashionable restaurants offering the kind of imaginative, artisanal cuisine we take for granted today were few and far between. In an article in *The Boston Globe* years later, a regular customer of the Pudding's described it as "the Ritz of Cambridge"—a phrase befitting its festive place in the community.

The building consisted of three stately floors: on the first, the Members' Lounge and the Hasty Pudding Theatre; on the second, the Club Bar; and on the third, the dining room and kitchen of the restaurant. As in an English country house, the layout contained an elaborate social choreography, an "upstairs-downstairs" feeling, though in this case the people *downstairs* had all the power.

A review in *The Boston Globe* once described the experience of dining at the Pudding as "stepping into the third installment of *Brideshead Revisited*." The comment was not far off, and indeed, the Halloween I was nine years old I went trick-or-treating as Sebastian's youngest sister, Cordelia Flyte, in a rust-colored taffeta party dress and with stiff black velvet bows wound round my pigtails. This was not at all that different from the way I dressed the rest of the year.

The Pudding, in any event, was of another era and in the shabby high-prep style. Hanging on the wall above the sofa outside the Club Bar was a dusty gold plaque reading FROM THE PUDDING TO THE PRESIDENCY, and below that were photographs of all the U.S. presidents who had belonged to the Club: John Adams, John Quincy Adams, Theodore Roosevelt, Franklin Delano Roosevelt, and John F. Kennedy. Some of the framed theatrical posters of old Hasty Pudding shows dated back to the eighteenth century. The all-male Harvard a cappella group the Krokodiloes practiced in the Members' Lounge, and at any hour of the day the sounds of young male voices chirping the lyrics to show tunes could be heard soaring to those magical domed ceilings.

When you live in a college town, everybody knows that September is the true beginning of the new year. Come fall, I used to watch with sadness as the undergraduates bounded back into the building and made it their own again. The Hasty Pudding kids smashed our wineglasses and downed our liquor and, at the members' luncheons my parents cooked for, wolfed down helpings of fettuccine Alfredo without saying thank you. When cooking for the Hasty Pudding kids, my parents restricted the menu to simple things, like fettuccine Alfredo or maybe lamb chops, because, as my father muttered, "WASPs. They have no taste buds." I could picture the boys as they would be in middle age, dull and purplish from too much drinking. The girls had that rawboned, ash-blond look one sees so much of in New England. But on Strawberry Night—the night of the annual drag show for which the club was famous— furs came out of musty closets and diamonds sparkled on skin that was magically tanned from midwinter jaunts to Bermuda or Belize. One year, Rita Hayworth's step-granddaughter, Princess Zahra Aga Khan, was the president of the Club. My mother once got a check from her, signed simply *Princess Zahra*. We marveled at the high glamour of that.

According to legend, the building was also populated with the ghosts of Hasty Pudding Club members past: some spoke of several young men who had drowned on the *Titanic* swooping through the long muslin-curtained windows to haunt the dining room. I sometimes felt just a hint of them while watching the antique-yellow candlesticks softening down, to one day vanish.

For a long time, I assumed that bow ties—not regular ties—were the usual thing for men to wear. Only when I was a teenager did I realize that I had it wrong, for in Harvard Square, home of J.Press and the Andover Shop, bow ties *were* the usual thing.

Blame it on the Krokodiloes, who every Sunday brunch appeared in the dining room to entertain the guests with a medley of songs. The Krokodiloes specialized in pop music from the twenties to the fifties. Their bow ties came in bright colors—canary yellow or billiard green—and were tied perkily underneath their starched collars. Other identifiable characteristics of this tribe were freshly shined penny loafers, no facial hair, and a general shortness. They also shared mannerisms: the cock of the head, as if to catch an admiring glance; the merry patter of their feet against the brick sidewalks; the legs that seemed, tucked into belted khakis, not to stroll but to flounce.

In my earliest childhood, I saw "the Kroks," as everyone referred to them, all around the building. I saw them lounging on the steps in black tie. I heard them singing, their high-pitched, prissy voices carrying from the Members' Lounge to the dining room. Later in my life, when the Pudding opened for Sunday brunch, the Kroks became a weekly fixture as my mother asked them to perform in the dining room as a novelty. The Harvard alumni who dined at the Pudding loved the Krokodiloes because they reminded them of their college days.

So every Sunday brunch, they appeared without warning. Between twelve thirty and one o'clock, when the dining room was full of customers and the kitchen was turning out dozens of orders of shirred eggs and oysters Rockefeller, no one was safe. Popping out from underneath empty tables or from behind the waiters' station, they sprinted across the dining room, weaving between tables and winking at customers. They pranced and pranced, their penny loafers pointed in the air, until they formed, one by one, a semicircle in front of the bar. Every year, without fail, they recruited one member who was taller and gangly to stand in the center of the front row and introduce the group to the audience.

"Hello, I'm Chip," he would say, and point to the boy on his left, who bowed accordingly. "And this is Preston. And we are the Harvard Krokodiloes!"

Then the tall Krok would step back, and the short ones all spread out to make room for him. A reverent silence followed, and suddenly they would snap their fingers. *"The house, the house,"* they'd begin in their falsettos, *"the house of blue lights."* Between songs, they talked to the audience. "Now Johnny is a young man from—Yale," the tall one would say, prefacing the song "Johnny O'Connor," while the rest of them would all cover their mouths and cough at the mention of Yale. In between "Johnny O'Connor" and "Danny Boy," he would say, "Now the Harvard Krokodiloes

would like to take this opportunity to introduce themselves," which meant that they all shook their neighbors'
hands as the customers guffawed.

The Kroks' three most common varieties of music were
1930s show tunes, 1950s doo-wop numbers, and old Irish
songs. "Danny Boy" belonged to the latter category, and it
called for a solo. One of the short Kroks replaced the tall
one up front as the others hummed soulfully in the background. When he bowed, tears sparkled on his lashes—
whether from his immersion in the song or his delight in his
soprano, no one could tell.

"Runaway," one of the doo-wop tunes, always closed the
show. "The Harvard Krokodiloes would like to perform a
dance duo in the famed style of Fred Astaire and Ginger
Rogers," the tall one would say. "We hope you find it
delightful, and yet somehow artsy and pretentious." Two
Krokodiloes, usually the tall one and another short one,
acted out the lyrics, in which a jilted lover wonders where
his baby has gone. The short one played the love object.
He batted his eyelashes and sashayed around the dining
room as if his khakis had turned into a hoopskirt. In the
background, the other Krokodiloes timed their finger snaps
to their jumps while the two stars waltzed together. Finally,
the tall one lifted the short one in the air, and applause
swelled to the ceiling.

"The Kroko*dildo*es," the staff called the Krokodiloes, as in, "Fuck, the Krokodildoes are coming! The Krokodildoes are coming!" They ruined service for the rest of the afternoon, because they always blocked the waiters' station and, in the midst of their antics, no one could safely cross the dining room. Dishes stacked up on the butcher block and behind the bar and got confused with other ones.

Meanwhile, the customers—many of whom, as Harvard alumni, had enjoyed the performance—left poor tips, because their entrees had arrived late. One bartender got back at the Krokodiloes the only way he knew how: he tossed champagne corks at them in the middle of their performances, and it was a wonder, he assured me, that he had never thrown knives instead.

My older brother, Benjamin, and I both showed a healthy distrust of the Harvard Krokodiloes from an early age. But Mary-Catherine was rather fond of them and had the poor judgment to ask them to sing "Happy Birthday" to me one year. Some of the chefs came out of the kitchen to watch this most extraordinary performance, in which I actually had to sit, under extreme duress, on one of the Kroks' khaki-covered knees in the middle of the dining room.

During the summer the Krokodiloes went on world tours, and in the fall they returned, never taller, never older, and, no matter where they had traveled, never tanned. On went the bow ties and the navy blazers, as if they had never known any place except Cambridge in the autumn. When I walked through Harvard Yard, I saw signs for auditions posted on the bulletin boards, and on what always seemed like the first cold night of September I sat at a table in the dining room, doing my homework, and heard male voices float up from the Club Bar. They sang "The Way We Were" or "You're the Top" or "That's Entertainment." On my way to the bathroom, I passed the boys on the sofa, where, sipping their ginger ales, they all looked fresh out of prep school. The new Krokodiloes were recruited, but come Sunday brunch I could never tell the new faces from the old.

The grand event of every winter was meeting the movie stars. Every January, the Hasty Pudding Club elected the Man and Woman of the Year, and in February the two movie stars came to Cambridge to accept the awards. It was, for Harvard, a recent tradition: Woman of the Year dated back to 1951, and Man of the Year started in 1967. Downstairs, on the wall outside the doors to the theatre, the Hasty Pudding Club had mounted two wooden plaques with the names of all the winners in gold cursive, and they looked nearly as old as the FROM THE PUDDING TO THE PRESIDENCY plaque above the sofa. Only when you read the names of twentieth-century celebrities did you discover the truth.

Everyone swapped stories about the stars. Legend had it that when Elizabeth Taylor had accepted her award in the seventies, she had ditched the Hasty Pudding members and smoked on the back fire escape with the members of the Cambridge Fire Department. Later, when my parents should have failed their safety inspection because they had no emergency exit in the dining room, the head of the fire department passed them, because he forever associated the Hasty Pudding Club with giving him the chance to meet Elizabeth Taylor. My mother was sad that she didn't get to meet her; it was one of the great joys of her life when one of the bartenders told her she was "just like a blond Liz Taylor."

Meanwhile, Benjamin was the envy of all the boys at school when Sylvester Stallone was the Man of the Year in 1986 and he got to pose for photographs with him in front of the bar. The photographs show my brother, aged nine, standing up to Stallone's shoulder.

The year my parents opened the restaurant, Ella Fitzgerald was Woman of the Year. One of the chefs' wives had agreed to help out at the Pudding on her birthday so she could meet her, but after the wife had rolled pasta dough and shelled peas for hours, Ella had still not been introduced, and she flung her apron on the floor and drove home. Just then, Ella Fitzgerald herself swept into the kitchen and asked, "Where's Pat? I heard it's her birthday. I wanted to sing her a little song." Since *Pat* was a unisex name, her husband raised his hand, and Ella Fitzgerald sang "Happy Birthday" to *him* behind the line, to the great exasperation of his wife when she later heard the story.

There were other tales, other movie stars. Cher received a belt made out of rhinestone-studded pheasant feet from one of the line cooks and wore it for the rest of the night; Clint Eastwood wore a three-piece brown suit, which my mother later told reporters was "the most confident fashion statement I've ever seen"; Harrison Ford, when asked if he thought any of the Hasty Pudding kids had a future in Hollywood, rubbed his eyes and said, "They're . . . energetic, I guess"; Meg Ryan chewed gum at the dinner table.

The Woman of the Year arrived in the afternoon, and every year I skipped school to attend the ceremony. In her honor, the Hasty Pudding Club organized a parade down Holyoke Street, in which one of the boys donned a wig and pretended to pass for the actress, who followed him in the next float. The actress almost always wore an Armani pantsuit in the afternoon and a slinky black dress for dinner. Perhaps because it was Harvard's version of the Oscars and not Hollywood's, she would seldom wear jewelry, and never furs. Her black peacoat, which she would toss in the office so nobody would steal it, always had Italian labels and came in too thin a wool for the New England winter.

The Woman of the Year ate dinner at the Pudding; the Man was taken out to eat at a different place every year (whatever happened to be the most fashionable restaurant of the moment). The menu varied according to the star's diet (my father dreaded having to cater to vegetarians), but the Club specified that we serve hasty pudding and vanilla ice cream for dessert. "The poor suckers, they swear by that goddamn gruel," I had heard my father say. "It's like something the fucking Pilgrims ate." Hasty pudding, a pudding or porridge of grains cooked in milk or water, was indeed a cheerless dish dating back to sixteenth century England.

The Man of the Year received his award on Strawberry Night, the opening night of the drag show. Every year I went to Strawberry Night, and every year the usher sniffed at my ticket marked "Upstairs at the Pudding—Comped" and led me to the second-to-last row of seats. The burgundy leather seats were shabby and too small. The theatre always felt hot, even in February. Two undergraduates introduced the movie star, and then forced him, as in a hazing ritual, to strap a bra over his tuxedo. He then grinned when they handed him his Pudding Pot while photographers snapped pictures.

Like the Krokodiloes' routines, the drag show never changed. The characters always included a selection of strumpets, an indignant queen who got to wear a hoopskirt, and a nurse who twitched her hips underneath a white pencil skirt; the story took them to the far corners of the globe and involved men in red military jackets with swords; to sing on key did not matter, as long as they enunciated the puns; and the show was long. An hour and a half later, the curtain dropped at intermission.

For the next half hour, the Man of the Year lounged in the empty dining room, and that was where we finally met him. He seemed, no matter who he was and no matter how buoyant he had appeared onstage, rumpled and vague. He yawned as he signed people's playbills and autograph books, and asked the nearest staff member if he could use a bathroom. Afterward, the movie star fiddled with the rickety lock of the kitchen bathroom and staggered, as if to the gallows, three flights down to the theatre to watch the rest of the show.

Every Man and Woman of the Year received a Pudding Pot, a fat, gilt pot with their name and the year of the award carved into it in cursive letters. I wondered what they did with them afterward—if they placed them next to their Oscars, or if, as Michelle Pfeiffer was discovered to have done, they left them behind in their rooms at the Charles Hotel.

Sometimes I closed my eyes and tried to imagine the Pudding Pot in a Hollywood home, but in my mind it never made it to the West Coast. It stayed behind, on a pink linen tablecloth at 10 Holyoke Street, Cambridge, in the heart of Harvard Square.

Two

FRONT ROOM
vs. KITCHEN

$\mathscr{I}$n the beginning, my father was the head chef and my mother made the desserts. Mary-Catherine ran the dining room and greeted customers.

Until I was six years old, we lived in a rambling white farmhouse in Bedford on a piece of land called Dudley Road. There my mother used to watch my brother and me while making the desserts for the restaurant. In the yellow French country kitchen of the farmhouse, she stood at the table wearing a coarse white apron over her pink-and-green Shetland sweater. The charlottes cooled in their tin molds while she squeezed lemons and crushed strawberries to flavor her Sicilian ices. The juices trickled into the rectangular tins she stored them in. Then she split off a sheet of foil and smoothed it out on top of the tins; the foil crackled beneath her hands.

Later on, the names of the desserts she made got printed in dark green cursive on the backs of the menus: *Raspberry*

Fool. Queen Mother's Cake with a Shot of Rum. Mocha Ice Parfait in a Bitter-Chocolate Tuille. And, of course, *Charlotte au Chocolat.*

Every day, come late afternoon, we would drive the desserts my mother had made at home to the restaurant. We had to get there by five o'clock at the latest, because the prep staff needed to unload and plate the desserts before customers arrived for their reservations starting at six. My mother carried the desserts out to the car and I carried the decorations, the meringue mushrooms and pouches of coconut shavings. We also made sure to bring a party dress for me to change into later on; little girls could not be seen in the dining room in just *anything*.

My mother's car was always full of too many things. But somehow she arranged it so that all of the desserts would fit. She hurled my party dress, cocooned in a layer of plastic, on top of the desserts. I held her pocketbook in my lap, and between my feet on the floor I gripped bottles of champagne.

On the ride there, she told me, "Memorize everyone's name. The waiters, the busboys, the dishwashers, everyone. You don't say just 'Thank you,' you say 'Thank you' and then the person's name. It's bad manners if you don't."

"Yes, Mummy."

"And you look into the waiters' eyes when they're taking

your order," she went on, "and you thank them when they do anything, even when it's just refilling your water glass, and even if they've already done it a half dozen times that night."

I sighed. "Yes, Mummy."

My mother had gained weight since having me, but her face was still beautiful, the brows fine and the nose uptilted like a doll's. Once upon a time, at boarding school, she'd been voted both "Best Manners" and "Prettiest Girl."

We got to the city—that meant Harvard Square. Harvard Square had redbrick sidewalks and it smelled like cigarettes. Pedestrians tossed quarters at street performers and homeless people slept on the grates. There were a lot of them in those days. My mother parked in the lot behind the Hasty Pudding Club, where my father had parked his car in the morning. The Dumpster reeked of last night's red wine and Roquefort flan, and ivy straggled down the back of the redbrick building. The chefs smoked on the fire escape. The chefs in those days were always smoking, always and everywhere. They waved to us, and we both waved back, saying, "Hello, hello," in voices that people called "chirpy." My mother propped open the steel door with a milk crate. Then we marched back to the car, lifted the desserts into our arms, and lugged them up the stairs. There were so many desserts to carry that this always took us several trips.

The stairs leading to the kitchen festered with filth. They stank of eggs and rotted red meat and the cigarette stubs the chefs had mashed into the concrete with the soles of their sneakers. The only light reaching the stairs filtered through the ivy-shaded windows with wrought-iron bars. "Don't look down," she said. "Don't look." We never said that word: *rats*. Not even the other word: *mice*. We were both deathly afraid of rodents.

The kitchen was large and drafty, and over the last century its white walls had blurred to a sooty gray. Black rubber mats stuck to the linoleum floor. A single butcher block, smudged with flour, ran down the line. Copper pots hung from the rack on the ceiling. Tupperware containers lined the walls and were labeled in red Magic Marker with the poetic names of various herbs, mushrooms, lettuces: CHICORY. TRUMPETS OF DEATH. RADICCHIO. Dust gathered in the corners between the stoves and the refrigerators. Once again, I feared the sight of rodents.

My father stood at the head of the line—that meant he got to handle the meat. Everyone else did vegetables or pasta, and then there was the prep person, who decorated the entree with flecks of fried sage and who checked to make sure the dollops of sauce hadn't smeared on the plate. My father's hands pounded a slab of tenderloin.

My father was a big man, broad-shouldered, soft-bellied,

from German immigrant stock in Chicago. His full head of curly brown hair was already turning gray. But where gray hair gave some men distinction, it gave him a faintly frazzled, electrified quality, an effect heightened by the flecks of ash that were forever falling from his cigarette onto his thin black T-shirt. This was before the days when young chefs just out of culinary school insisted on getting their own chef's whites. I'd only ever seen my father put on his chef's jacket when he was photographed for a picture accompanying an article or a review, and then he did not look quite like himself.

My mother ripped the tinfoil off the desserts, revealing what was underneath. The staff flocked to the cold station, as they always did when we brought the desserts. They shared spoonfuls of melted lemon ice (people in kitchens have no qualms about sharing food—family-style, my mother called this way of eating). But my father stayed behind the line, a cigarette dangling between his lips; he preferred savory foods to sweet.

When I was a small child, I associated my parents with individual flavors. It was the same way you might filter someone through a prism of color—thinking of some people in blues, other people in reds—but instead of color, the sensation I latched on to was flavor. My mother's flavors were always those of the desserts she made—suave caramels and milk chocolates and the delicate, utterly feminine accents of crystallized violets or buttery almonds. But my father's flavors—my father's flavors were something else altogether. They were subtle and elusive and melted on the tongue only to vanish before you could place them. Dark, adult flavors, and slightly bitter: veal carpaccio, silvery artichokes. And, most of all, mushrooms: chanterelles, chicken of the woods, and—my father's favorite mushroom of all— trumpets of death.

"Oh, look," said my mother, glancing at her watch. "Charlotte, go on, get dressed before the customers come."

It was half past five. The "front of the house" had been at the restaurant since three, freshening flower arrangements and changing the pink linens, and now they had to change into their uniforms. I had to change, too, into what was essentially *my* uniform as a child: a party dress. I pushed open the black-painted double doors of the kitchen and walked out into the dining room. A candle sparkled on every table, and the carpet had just been vacuumed. The ceiling with its white beams sprawled as high and wide as the kitchen's. The lights from the pewter chandeliers threw shadows on the posters from the Hasty Pudding Club, paintings done in all the rich, dull shades my mother had told me that as blondes we could never wear—crimsons and hunter greens and burnished golds—paintings of court jesters and skulls and crocodiles, and of tufted satin balloons sailing into a night sky.

I moved fast, because soon the waiters would be undressed. We had only one public bathroom at the Pudding, and it was unisex, but only the waitresses changed there. The waiters used to peel off their clothes in the middle of the dining room. Some men had hair on their chests and some men did not. Some men wore boxers in solid colors, others wore patterns, like apple blossoms against a cream backdrop. ("Why is it the gay guys always have the best boxers?" I'd heard my mother remark, to no one in particular.) And some men didn't wear boxers at all: they wore plain white briefs.

The bathroom on the second floor had blue walls, and the stall doors rattled and shook. Mice darted behind the toilets, and to make the toilets flush you jerked a rusty chain in back. The white porcelain sinks were cracked and stained with brown; I'd heard my father say that the members of the Hasty Pudding Club had been vomiting into them for the past hundred years.

By the time I got there, most of the waitresses had their tops off. Some of them wore black lace bras, which meant they had to change into pastel ones because the black showed through their white shirts. White shirts and black pants: that was the uniform. This was before you ever saw waiters wearing plain black T-shirts instead of white shirts, before bottled still water was offered and not tap, before olive oil and not butter came with every bread basket. At the Pudding, the shirts the waitresses wore varied: blouses that plunged past the breasts and wrapped around the waist; blouses with gathered sleeves and Peter Pan collars; blouses trimmed with black velvet or jazzed up with rhinestone buttons. The waiters all wore the same basic white shirt. For color, they added satin cummerbunds or bow ties.

"Let me see your dress," the waitresses said. "Such a pretty dress." They fastened the hooks and closed the zippers and tied the sashes around my waist. I tightened the straps of my Mary Janes and skittered upstairs, past the overstuffed burgundy leather sofa on the landing where customers sat sipping Scotch-and-sodas before dinner. The waiters were all dressed now. "Let me see your dress," they said, and I dropped my arms to my sides and stood up straight (as my mother had instructed me, saying "Posture is everything"). "Such a pretty dress."

For the rest of the night, I had to figure out how to entertain myself. Everyone else was busy. My father was behind the line and Benjamin was in the kitchen, too, where he liked to hang out with the guys. My mother was fluttering from one point of focus to another, expediting appetizers, plating desserts, solving problems. Mary-Catherine was greeting and soothing customers. So, with all of this activity swirling around me, I had dinner at a table in the dining room by myself. The dining room at the Pudding was vast, and in those days, before restaurants were so fashionable and before so many people went out to eat, the room was only ever full on Saturday nights.

I sat at a four-top known as "A-1," or, occasionally, "Family Table." The table, the very first one you saw when you walked through the double doors of the dining room, was not considered to be a desirable one for paying customers. Waiters crashed there at the ends of their shifts to talk to me and to nurse a glass of wine. My mother and Mary-Catherine sat there during the daytime to pay the bills, and my father to do the ordering from the vendors. When, on those busy Saturday nights, customers sat there instead, I felt unanchored, adrift without A-1, and would wander around the whole restaurant seeking a steady perch from which to sit back and watch all of the bustle.

As soon as I sat down at the table, the bartender made my Shirley Temple. The martini glass teetered on the edge of the tray. When my waiter handed me the glass, the darker pink of the liquid splashed onto the lighter pink of the tablecloth. Maraschino cherries rimmed the orange slice floating in the center and the grenadine tinted the ice cubes pink. I swallowed the beverage fast and waited for the waiter to come back to the table so I could ask for another one. Until then, I coiled the cherry stems around my fingers and wondered what to do for the rest of the evening, after all three courses. Maybe I could play the piano in the Club Bar. Or relight the candles for the eight o'clock seating; my mother let me help with that sometimes. Or I could try to chase the Pudding ghost—the staff claimed it lived inside the poster over the waiters' station, the one of the scowling gray-faced man with the black top hat and red fangs.

Time passed, and my courses arrived. On a typical night at the Pudding, I might order an appetizer of shrimp rolled in brown-butter bread crumbs on skewers, so the oil wouldn't spread on your hands. For an entree: squab with black lentils and bacon, only in the pink light of the dining room the lentils weren't black, but blue—a deep, inky blue. And for dessert, I might ask for my favorite treat: candied violets on a lace doily. My teeth cracked open each crystalline blossom, and I could smell the sheets of wax paper they came in mingled with the sugar.

Sometimes, when I was at the Pudding on Saturday afternoons, I would steal candied violets from the cold station when no one was looking. You had to be quick about it, so no one would see. I'd open the tab of one of the little pansy-purple boxes with the French words on it and stick my hand between the sheets of wax paper and pluck a violet or two. But I wouldn't eat the violets right away. I'd save them and eat them a little later, so I could let the flower shape slacken and the crystals melt on my tongue.

I got up from the table and walked over to the door in the far corner of the dining room, which had a stairwell leading to the Club Bar. We used the Club Bar for private parties, while the Hasty Pudding Club kids used it for luncheons and other Club events. The staircase had a black banister with white legs. The floor was black-and-white, too, a pattern I had heard my mother call "diamond." The walls, except for the white wainscoting, were red, and they were sprinkled with more posters like the ones upstairs. A rusted poker leaned against the edge of the fireplace. Ashes collected behind the grate, and pink roses rotted in a vase on top of the mantel.

On the wall above the fireplace, the Hasty Pudding members had mounted three stuffed crocodiles: two grown ones and a baby. These were the crocodiles that the Krokodiloes were named for. Teddy Roosevelt had shot them on one of his hunting trips. One time I stood on a chair on my tiptoes and tried to touch the crocodiles, to see if they were really dead, if they wouldn't bite, but when I stroked the crinkled scales of the baby's tail, I lost my nerve and dropped my hands to my sides. Despite having been dead for almost a hundred years, those crocodiles were still menacing. Their eyes, sunk in the stiff green flesh, glowed dully, and their yellowed teeth showed in their open mouths.

Looking for something to do to pass the time, I unbuckled the clasps of my Mary Janes. After the last private party, the waitstaff had pushed all the chairs against the walls, and there was plenty of room for me to dance. The velvet of the crimson rugs had thinned over the years, and the gold tassels wiggled when I moved my feet. I wanted to hear music. But the piano, situated against the ivy-trimmed window, was broken. When I touched the keys, dust wafted into my face and quavering chords sounded in the room, then died.

After dancing, I decided to go upstairs to take a nap underneath the bar. We didn't have a real bar, just a long oak table in the corner of the room draped with a pink linen tablecloth and covered with glasses and bottles and old-fashioned black-pepper grinders. Underneath were crates of champagne with bundles of linen stuffed between the empty spaces. I scrambled under the flap of the tablecloth and tried to arrange myself on top of the clutter.

I swaddled myself in some of the tablecloths; a wrapped bundle of linen served as a pillow. Underneath the bar it was dark, and the carpet felt as soft as my holiday muff; I could trace the flecks of gold with my fingers. As ice cubes tinkled and cocktail shakers rattled above me, I rubbed my nose in the linens, breathing in the scent of starch. The sounds of the restaurant faded. I could barely hear the murmur of the customers' conversations or the scuff of the waiters' shoes on the carpet, and finally I fell asleep.

Hours later, my mother stooped down and tapped me on the puffed sleeve of my party dress. I got up from underneath the bar, rubbing my eyes, only to discover that in the time since I had fallen asleep, the dining room had been completely transformed. All of the customers were gone and, as at the end of a play, the lights were on. You could see how shabby the room was now; you could see the chips of paint missing in the wainscoting and the soft, misty cobwebs on the chandeliers. The waiters were undressing now, as they had at the beginning of the evening, before service. They stood around in various states of undress, in boxers or blue jeans and black turtlenecks. Everyone drank beer or ate scoops of mocha ice out of wineglasses. That was a signature dessert of my mother's, almost as good as charlotte au chocolat. Anyone who was hooked on caffeine *and* had a sweet tooth couldn't get enough of it. "This is like crack," the waitresses would say, cramming another spoonful in their mouths. Meanwhile, there was always one person who was assigned to sit at A-1 and count out the money. I knew better than to bother the person with the money.

Where did the waiters keep all that money? I wondered, looking at all those rustling green bills. I knew that most of them would spend at least some of it tonight. Restaurant people always get this buzz of fresh energy after a shift. They go out for more drinks, and you might think they'd be so used to fine dining that they'd go to fancy places, but no—they'd go to The Tasty, which was the best option for restaurant people because it was open twenty-four hours a day. And what one craved after a busy night was honest food, cut with grease: life-affirming animal grease. Ending a shift was like coming to earth after waking up with a hangover. My father swore by The Tasty's fried-egg sandwich.

"Hits the spot, Char," he'd say. And then he'd light up another cigarette.

The whole world, my mother said, was divided into front room people and kitchen people. Kitchen people despised slow nights, smoked, and drank beer. They smoked behind the line, and it was like watching a magic trick, how the ashes trembled above freshly primped plates and yet never landed. A kitchen person could work in the front room, but if they did, they sponged off the martini glasses themselves and checked on the other waiters' tables, just to give themselves something else to do. Front room people were noted for their ability to put on a good show in public.

Mary-Catherine was the ultimate front room person. She had a big smile, curly brown hair, and almost always wore the color red, which was her color, just as my mother's color was pink. On Saturday nights, she wore high-necked cream silk blouses and flowing skirts of black or crimson velvet. Mary-Catherine loved chamber music, croquet, Victorian novels, and tea parties, and so her tastes were perfectly in keeping with the old-world atmosphere of the dining room. Watching her lead the dining room like a conductor leads an orchestra, I marveled at how she could remember so many different customers' names and their favorite wines and dishes. She was deft at smoothing out difficult situations and erasing hard feelings. Her apology letters—written in response to the occasional complaint letter—were so lushly, artfully apologetic that, my father remarked, "Christ, by the time customers are done reading them, they practically feel like they should write an apology letter to *her.*"

If Mary-Catherine was the ultimate front room person, Jake was, to my mind, the ultimate kitchen person. He had worked behind the line since opening night, and I had heard my father tell my mother, "That kid never misses a day's work, but Jesus Christ, there are days I wish he would." Jake wore a duct-taped leather jacket and a purple sequined pheasant-foot earring in one ear, and he played in a punk-rock band. His skateboard had stickers of skeletons pasted on it. "Fuck! Fuck! Fuck!" he sometimes said, splitting arti-choke hearts open with a scalpel.

Benjamin was close to Jake, who had taught him how to skateboard. But I was deathly afraid of him.

One time Jake brought a gun to work. My father said it was because he was high on quaaludes, and he worried that Jake would pull the trigger in the middle of the eight o'clock rush. So my father stuffed a fifty-dollar bill in the pocket of his chef's pants, walked downstairs to the first floor, knocked on the door of the Members' Lounge, and bribed one of the Hasty Pudding undergraduates to buy the gun from Jake. "You'll never believe it," Jake told the chefs later. "So one of these little Pudding kids wanted my gun . . . I took him for all he was worth."

Another time, when the Rockettes performed in the the-atre, Jake cornered one of them in the downstairs hallway and asked if she could give him a private show. Soon the whole group accompanied her into the dining room. The Rockettes twirled and kicked their famous legs up in the air while Jake, still in his chef's whites, perched himself on top of the bar and clapped.

He also got into fights behind the line. My father had hired a Harvard student, the offspring of one of the richest banking families in the country, who wanted to rebel by working in a kitchen; he had shown up for his interview dressed in head-to-toe chef's whites and carrying his own set of knives. When the banking heir, idling behind the line, called Jake's risotto "soggy," Jake pulled one of the kid's own butcher knives on him. "Didn't think you'd ever get these bloody, huh?" he said. "Think again!" And he grabbed him by the collar of his monogrammed chef's coat before my father separated them.

Jake dated Sarah, who worked plating my mother's pastries in the cold station. Sometimes I plopped myself between Sarah and Jake on the butcher block when they drank their beers during breaks. Sarah's platinum curls stuck to the back of her neck, and a single black bra strap slithered over her tanned shoulder. At the end of the night, they went home together. Jake had a motorcycle he parked against the Dumpster, and Sarah pounced on the back, shaking out her curls, as the bike thundered out of the alley. Neither of them wore a helmet.

Carla was another kitchen person, but she was a kitchen *woman*—my mother said that was a very special thing. She stood six feet tall from her charcoal-caked white high-top sneakers to the top of her dark brown buzz cut, and she stored a pack of Marlboro Reds in the olive-green T-shirt she wore every day. The elastic had collapsed around the neck and cuffs, and when she moved behind the line, I could tell she didn't wear a bra. I thought she didn't have any manners, either.

"You," she said to me, "go out in the dining room and count how many poor suckers are left. I'll personally drool on their cheese platters if they don't hurry it up." When a recipe called for alcohol, she always swigged some from the bottle, and drops of sherry or Chianti splashed on her T-shirt as well as in the pan. "Blood and booze," she said, stirring the boiling red juices in the pan with her fingers. "Blood and booze, that's what they pay for."

Carla used the back stairs to the building and refused to go in the dining room during service. Every time she used her employee gift certificates, she wore the same mauve housedress with her white high-tops. "I just don't have any other shoes," she told me when I visited her at her table. "Do you think it's okay? You can't see a thing through all these damn linens." She dined alone, and she lived alone, too, except for her two dogs, Benny and Sadie. Sadie was a black Doberman, blind, and Benny was a brown one with a bullet in his leg. At staff lunch, she entertained us with the dreams she had had about Benny and Sadie.

"I had another dream about bridges last night," she said,

while bottles of Chianti popped open around the table. Carla was terrified of heights; even fire escapes scared her. "I was going over the Brooklyn Bridge and Benny and Sadie were with me. Sadie was driving." Everyone knew that Sadie was the blind one. "And they were talking, but that didn't make any sense, because *Benny* was talking, too. Sadie does talk—I mean, she talks to *me*—but Benny never does." With this, she downed her Chianti.

Front room people smoked and drank, too. But they held their cigarettes differently, delicately, and they liked drinks with fancy names. Sometimes, after the customers had left, Patrick opened bottles of a green liquid called Chartreuse, which matched the color of the rhinestones on his cat-eye glasses. He tied paisley scarves around his neck, and he wore a plaid kilt and combat boots to one of the Christmas parties. His guests wore kilts and combat boots, too. "Charlotte, don't stare," my mother told me; but I noticed all the kitchen people did.

Patrick was a hairdresser during the day and a bartender at night. He did not like the way my mother styled my hair, in two balls on the sides of my head that were forever slipping out of their bobby pins, and he told me, "Think glamorous." During setup, I sat down on a barstool and Patrick yanked a brush through my hair and spread gel through my bangs. The morning of the first-grade Christmas pageant, he did my makeup: silver eye shadow, thick mascara, red lipstick. My teacher told me to wipe it off—shepherds didn't wear silver eye shadow—and after that, whenever Patrick took out the hairbrush, I scrambled underneath the bar.

Richard waited tables at night so he could still write poems. People couldn't write poems, he told me, if they had a real job. I knew what *real jobs* meant: you got Saturday nights off. I couldn't picture Richard at a real job, in a suit and tie. He had a curly ponytail that was already graying, and Birkenstocks. "Miss Charlotte," he called me. "Hello, Miss Charlotte."

During setup, and on the slow nights during the summer, Richard told me stories about the Hasty Pudding Theatricals posters. He was tall and could touch the posters, but I squinted whenever he pointed at the illustrations. The posters showed the Lady of Loravia, who capped her raven bob in a gold crown and had sad eyes; a crocodile curled in a ball and flicking his tongue; men in brightly colored tights, stalking around a bonfire and thrusting spears into the air; and, of course, the man with the fangs and the top hat. The paper had crinkled and grayed until it matched the color of his skin, and when Richard said the Pudding ghost lived inside the frame, I believed him.

"Sometimes he floats out of the frame," he told me. "He floats all over the dining room and down to the cellar, with the rats. He hides inside the stoves and under the tables and the sofa cushions and in the ice chest. He can fit anywhere he wants—he could even slip under the bar with *you*."

I shuddered. "But *no one else* can fit underneath the bar," I said. "Only me."

"Ghosts are different," Richard said. "They change shapes. I should know. I saw him once, out there."

He pointed past the windows on the left side of the dining room to the sagging roof where we stored milk crates and barstools and chilled bottles of champagne in the winter. My mother didn't let me go out there by myself; she said it was dangerous.

"He didn't look like a person," Richard said. "He had turned himself into a candle, moving back and forth in the air. When I saw him, all at once the candle blew out and died."

"Everyone else gets to see the Pudding ghost," I said. "Is it true it pulls the fire alarm on Saturday nights? And does it really make the dishwasher make all those horrible sounds before it breaks?"

Richard nodded. "And when the lights go off in the dining room—all of a sudden—who do you think is behind that?"

"My mother says the waiters should stop leaning on the light switch. She says front room people—"

"No, no," he said. "She just can't admit we have a ghost. It would be bad for business."

Sometimes, on breaks, Richard took me on errands in the Square. It was his job to pick up the staff take-out orders. We went to the Hong Kong on Mass Ave, where they served drinks called Scorpion Bowls in round, plunging glasses and the sign flashed red at night. I swiped pink-and-green soft-centered mints from a dish on the hostess's station and stared at the kernels of fried rice and Coca-Cola stains on the dark red carpet while Richard paid for the brown paper bags full of food. My mother told me not to eat that kind of food: "Never buy anything that ends in ninety-nine cents."

Richard liked to go to Harvard Book Store after we got the food, if we had time before the customers arrived. He liked the used section, downstairs. The shelves were covered with cutouts of pulp-fiction covers: women with tumbling hair and sticky lips, in bullet bras and stockings whose seams slunk down their legs. The men there carried leather bags with fraying shoulder straps, and tufts of white hair peeked out from their corduroy caps. Richard bought thin books of poetry for as little as twenty-five cents. I'd been to lunch at Richard's apartment, where he served me warmed artichokes and showed me his library of marvelous old books.

Kitchen people didn't get takeout at night. My mother said they didn't have the time. Sometimes, for staff lunch, they sent me down to Elsie's, the sandwich shop on the corner of Holyoke and Mount Auburn. Elsie's had no chairs or tables, just some stools at the counter. It always seemed like the fuse for the lights had blown. Grease sopped through the brown paper bags and onto my hands. It came from the pastrami: all the chefs ordered extra-thick pastrami sandwiches. "Best damn thing in the Square, that pastrami," my father said, ripping off the sheets of paper.

Kitchen people understood that food didn't have to be gourmet to taste good, and that sometimes gourmet food didn't taste good at all. "Kiwis are a soulless fruit," my mother once said when she saw them in a fruit tart on the Ritz's dessert tray. "Don't ever use sun-dried tomatoes," my father told his staff. "They'll take away your magic powers." Even junk food could be better. Once, for Jake's birthday, the staff laid out his favorite foods—frozen meatballs and Twinkies—on brass serving plates in the dining room. When they sliced the Twinkies horizontally to expose the cream, even my mother admitted they made an attractive dessert.

At staff Christmas parties we served junk food, too: sour-cream-and-onion potato chips, chicken wings, and hot dogs, and for dessert more Twinkies. The rest of the year I never ate food like that, and by the holidays Cotswold tarts and melon wrapped in prosciutto bored me. In my black velvet party dresses, I gnawed on fried drumsticks, with a napkin stuffed into my lace collars to catch the crumbs. "I'm not whipping up any foie gras for you tonight, kiddo," said Carla, who, in her olive-green T-shirt and holding a beer, looked the same as she did behind the line. "Fend for yourself."

The whole staff decorated the tree together. The restaurant owned few ornaments—some violet glass bulbs in various sizes, beaded cranberry sprigs, and a platinum-blond angel to pin on top—so every year the staff brought ornaments they had made themselves. One year Lydia, the line cook, outlined her expired Neiman Marcus charge card in red glitter; another year a waitress constructed a model of the Pudding staircase, complete with green velvet carpet, and the next year a model of a table with a pink linen tablecloth. There were rubber crocodiles dangling from strings, ropes of pop-bead pearls to loop around the branches, and a clean-picked cow rib spray-painted silver and dangling from a rhinestone hook. I decorated the lower half of the tree, the only part I could reach, while the adults decorated the top.

I don't remember Benjamin decorating the tree with me, or hanging out in the dining room at that party, although he must have been there, just as he doesn't figure into many of my memories of the Pudding. I expect he was in the kitchen, or maybe on the fire escape. My mother got it right after all: the world *was* divided into front room and kitchen people. I was the former and Benjamin was the latter. His memories of the Pudding from those early days probably would be of the rhythms and flavors of the kitchen, whereas mine were of the velvety dining room. Unlike me, Benjamin was a rugged and physical child, always building forts and climbing trees at our farmhouse and happy to help with shelling peas and rolling pasta at the Pudding. There is a black-and-white photograph my father must have taken of Benjamin and a cousin of ours stirring a pot of chocolate sauce in the kitchen of our farmhouse. No doubt that chocolate sauce was later drizzled over some exquisite dessert and served to a customer at the Pudding who never suspected that two young boys had played any part in its invention.

Three

SKINNED PEARS
& DEAD DUCKS

My parents were getting dressed to go to court. They stood at the foot of their bed at the farmhouse. It was a rare sight, seeing both of them home at the same time; my father worked such long days at the restaurant. My mother tossed an old tweed blazer on the bed while my father, who never wore anything but kitchen clothes, stood there with his hands in his pockets, looking deeply unhappy.

"This one," my mother said, gesturing to the blazer. "It's the only one."

My father sighed, and he could really *sigh* when he wanted to let you know he was fed up with something.

"What?" My mother threw up her hands. "It's *Harvard*. They'll all be wearing tweed."

So, I thought, that explained it. They were going to court with Harvard.

I think I was about six then, and it was the first time I ever heard the words *the lease*. Evidently, Harvard Real Estate was after possession of the building. They were battling with my parents about their right to extend their lease.

Eventually, my father put on the tweed blazer and my parents and Mary-Catherine went to court. They won the case. But I never did forget those words: *the lease*.

Meanwhile, on Dudley Road, stalks of rhubarb grew behind the blue-painted shed and roses bloomed on a bush above the cellar window. The swing set creaked. The stones in the garden path wobbled underneath my feet and there were pink sprigged cushions on the white wicker chairs on the porch. Inside, everything was pink and green, green and pink: the walls in my bedroom the color of the center of a raspberry thumbprint cookie, the floors the color of the sliver of green in after-dinner mints; the floor in my parents' bedroom the same, and the walls a smudged baby pink.

Something was always broken at the farmhouse, just as something was always broken at the restaurant. When you turned on the faucets, either the cold water or the hot water refused to flow. We hardly ever had enough hot water to fill the bathtub. During downpours, water flooded the basement, and when it snowed, chunks of snow slid off the roof and thudded to the ground, making the whole house rumble. We had no overhead lights, just lamps with rickety stems and rose-tinted shades, and often the electricity went out.

My mother lit candles then—pink candles, the same color as our living-room walls, and blue candles, the same blue as our kitchen sink with the cracks in the porcelain.

No one ever cleaned up. Even during the summer, my parents did not scoop out the ashes from behind the grate in the fireplace. The cashmere throws on the floor smelled of smoke, both from the ashes and from my father's cigarettes. The grease of bacon fat crusted the white rags my mother flung on the counters. There were cooking tools everywhere: paring knives for boning quails, truffle cutters, butcher knives to hack through cubes of dark chocolate, pans thick with grime.

My father always came home from the restaurant late; sometimes I was still awake and sometimes I was not. He brought home food—all the things in the cold room that would go bad if left until tomorrow—stalks of salsify my mother sauteed in lemon juice and sage; blackberries so ripe they verged on moldy; scraps of Dover sole wrapped in wax paper. Sometimes my mother served me the Dover sole on saltines, but my father didn't eat anything. He had eaten at the restaurant, he said. Then he lit a cigarette and locked the door to his darkroom where he printed and developed photographs all night long.

That was his other interest besides cooking: photography. He did platinum prints, which everyone said were very hard to do but made these magical melting shadows of silver on thin sheets of paper. There was one broom he took photographs of all the time: the same broom, again, and again, and again. And also one young woman who worked in the cold station at the restaurant plating desserts, who couldn't have been more than twenty or twenty-one and bore a striking resemblance to my mother. Whenever I came across a portrait of this young woman posing in profile, her fine, floaty blond hair grazing a bare shoulder, I would do a double take to convince myself that it was not my mother, who years ago had posed for him in the same ethereal style.

Sometimes, if it snowed, my parents closed the restaurant and my father stayed home. Then they cooked together— brioche was their favorite food to make: brioche doughnuts, brioche with bacon, brioche slathered in sweet butter and stuffed with fried oysters. But then the snow ceased, my father went back to the restaurant, and my mother and I stayed behind in the farmhouse, eating the loaves of brioche as long as they'd last.

It was a Saturday night; I was six years old. My mother and I sat at our usual table, A-1. Our entrees arrived: crab vicar for me, osso bucco for my mother. Crab vicar was actually an appetizer—crabmeat thick with hollandaise and rice and served on a bed of sea salt on top of a hollowed-out scallop shell. That and smoked pheasant with Roquefort flan were my favorite dishes on the menu. I ate my crabmeat and hoped that my mother would scoop out some of the marrow onto my bread plate; we usually shared food. But my mother, who had appeared in the dining room in her pink-and-green Shetland sweater and black "kitchen" pants, was not eating. She only peeled off the petals of the Roman artichokes with her fork, she who had taught me that playing with your food was bad manners. I opened my mouth to ask about the marrow when our waiter approached the table.

"Would you care for anything else?" he asked.

"No," my mother said, and I noticed she didn't add *thank you*. "We're done for tonight."

The waiter cleared our plates. I still held a forkful of crab vicar in my hand. It plopped onto the tablecloth. The rice scattered and the hollandaise stained the pink linen yellow. My mother toyed with a loose thread in her sweater.

"Go thank your father for dinner," she said. "Go, go behind the line."

I always thanked the chefs for dinner; that was good manners. "Go thank the kitchen," my mother had told me over and over again. *The kitchen,* she had said, but never *your father.* My parents raised me to believe that the help was more important than they themselves were.

I got up from the table and slipped into the kitchen. It was the end of the night; only the cold station was busy with people plating desserts, and I made my way to the head of the line, where my father usually stood. A hunk of prime rib still smoldered in a black pan. Cigarette ashes dappled the butcher block. But my father, my father wasn't *there.*

The next morning, I saw my mother crying in our kitchen at home. Her blond hair needed highlights and had tumbled out of its tortoiseshell combs. Flour had spilled onto the wood floor; I smelled lemon squares baking in the oven. Nobody had said the word *divorce,* but I knew. As I stared at my mother's body, rocking with sobs, I knew my father had gone.

"Come on," she said, rising and opening the door of the oven. "Time to take in the desserts to the restaurant." And then she said, "It's mine now."

Everyone had come to an agreement. From here on out, Mary-Catherine would continue to manage the dining room and my mother would take my father's place in the kitchen.

I watched my mother dress the night she took over the restaurant. She stood in her bedroom, struggling with the clasp of a caramel silk swing skirt. It didn't fit. She slipped the skirt off her hips and fumbled around in her closet until she settled on the navy circle skirt she had been wearing almost every day. It had three different hooks, she explained; she could still manage the loosest one.

She sighed. "I've got to," she said, as if to herself. "I've got to get my waist back, that's all there is to it."

That night, Benjamin and I stayed home with a babysitter. I tried to picture my mother at the head of the line, where my father had stood. But somehow, I couldn't.

The "head of the line" was then in my mind an exclusively male domain. Of course, this was true in most kitchens at the time, although I wouldn't necessarily have known that as a child. I only knew that I associated the position with my father, with meat and ashes and dodging the flames. My mother I associated with the softer, smoother flavors of the desserts she made, and with the landscape of our farmhouse—especially with the garden she loved, the pink and lavender candy-land of geraniums, peonies, and sweet peas.

But there was never to be another garden on Dudley Road. My parents' marriage had been deteriorating over the long winter, and by the time the spring came and the stalks of rhubarb were growing, I learned that we were going to lose the farmhouse. A developer had bought up the land surrounding Dudley Road, with plans to build condominiums on the property. Some of the other beautiful old houses were going to be bulldozed, but ours was going to be spared. Once we moved out of the house, it would be given a new paint job, new bathrooms, and new kitchen, and converted into an information center for prospective tenants.

It has always seemed to me, in memory, that my father up and left, vanished from our lives, that night at the Pudding when my mother told me to go say thank you to him and I couldn't find him behind the line. All I remember: the hunk of prime rib smoldering in a black pan. But that can't be right, or not entirely right. I think, now, that he must have come back sometime, if only to get his stuff—his cameras and platinum prints—from the farmhouse. And then there is this story I heard about the day we left Dudley Road. My father and a family friend of ours were ready to leave, thinking they'd taken care of everything, when the friend said, "Michael, what about the basement? Is there anything we should go get from down there?"

My father laughed and rolled his eyes. "Trust me," he said, "no way do you want to go *down to the basement.* Let's get out of this place."

For my father, a talented butcher, used to hang deer and other animals up to dry on our porch, and some of that meat, long forgotten, was stored in the basement of the farmhouse. They left; whatever game-meat delicacies that had been left to rot in the basement were discovered, presumably, when the renovations began.

My mother explained to me that my father didn't want to be a chef anymore. He'd lost interest in cooking, she said; he wanted to be an artist now.

After leaving us, he got a studio on the third floor of an old redbrick industrial building overlooking the commuter-rail tracks in Waltham. The first time I visited the building, he said to me, "There *is* an elevator, Char. But I wouldn't use it, if you know what I mean."

That whole building, I felt, was fragile, unstable. The steps trembled underneath my feet as we climbed the stairs, and the planks in the ceilings looked loose, as if flakes of sawdust would fall between the cracks. When we reached the third floor, my father told me, "Don't worry too much about the mice, Char. All of the lady painters have cats, wouldn't you know it?"

My father's studio was one vast room, with a ceiling almost as high as the one in the dining room at the Pudding. He had painted the walls silver leaf from top to bottom. His negatives dripped from a clothesline in the center of the room, and he had propped a moose head, drizzled with more silver leaf, on the wall. The moose's name, my father told me with a chuckle, was Ralph.

Taxidermy, later on when I was a grown-up, became

quite fashionable in certain circles. You would walk into chic restaurants and see animal heads mounted against a backdrop of carefully selected Victorian wallpaper. But it wasn't fashionable then. And I thought that this moose, Ralph, was absolutely ridiculous and absolutely terrifying. I thought *Ralph* was a stupid name, too. I glanced up at him, a child's judgment in my eyes.

My father's studio was cold. A mean wind whipped in through the holes in the windows, several of which, I noticed, were broken.

"That's because of the bar next door," my father said. "I think the customers get drunk and throw pebbles through the windows. I might patch those up with duct tape, one of these days."

I asked where the bathroom was.

"Oh, down the hall," he said. "We all share it. And hey, Char, check out the futon down there. If you want to sleep over, we can just drag it down the hall."

I walked down the hall. It felt windy in the bathroom, too. The walls were painted cornflower blue, and blobs of lavender wax stuck to the floor. The only block of soap on the sink was so soft and runny, it crumbled in my hands. I didn't see any towels.

Walking back to the studio, I stopped and looked at the

futon outside of the stall. It was smothered in dust, and I saw a smattering of stains from what looked like red wine. I didn't want to sleep there, or on the floor where the mice could get me. And if the mice did get me, I realized, it was unlikely that my father could be counted on to care.

But later that night, we ate herring on toast and marrons glacés in pools of heavy cream. And I curled up after all on that futon at the foot of my father's bed and drifted off to sleep.

What, for the record, did my father take photographs of? Chairs. Brooms. More chairs and brooms: hundreds of these, over the years. A skinned pear drowning in a puddle of silver leaf. Pigs' hooves, tipped with dried blood. In some photographs, the pigs' feet are arranged in almost coquettish poses, bringing to mind fractured female body parts. And then, he sometimes took pictures of his shoes. I remember one photograph of those old black slippers he used to wear, crisscrossed with duct tape. A dead duck, the crackly copper kind you sometimes see hanging by a string in the windows of Chinatown, is stuffed inside the shoe. Its head is flung back, and it looks like it's dying all over again.

hile the divorce was being finalized, we moved, for a year, to a rented Victorian house in another suburb. All that year, my mother ran the restaurant while also driving me to and from my private elementary school in Concord, and my brother to and from his school in Newton. But then because we could no longer afford the rent, we had to take in boarders, and then when we could no longer afford paying what we owed the private schools (even though we were both, at least partially, on scholarships), it was decided that we would move to Cambridge and both go to public school.

It must have been a dreadful day for my mother the first time she took us to see where we would be living. For one thing, the apartment was small: only a small living room, one bedroom, a study, and a kitchenette. Benjamin would sleep in a tiny loft. The study, where I was supposed to sleep, had no door. But worse, it was a *new* apartment. We both knew that, in New England, old was better. Old was cozy; old, like our farmhouse, like the Pudding, had magic and charm. This apartment, while perfectly livable, had none of that. Scratchy tan carpets stretched wall to wall, and the walls were a freshly painted white. The kitchenette had Formica countertops and tan-and-white tiles on the floor. I had heard my mother say she loathed carpeting, and most of all white walls.

The apartment was so small that even after we had moved many of our belongings from Dudley Road into storage, my mother being unable to part with anything, we still did not have nearly enough room for everything.

But she tried to be game about it. "It'll be just fine," she said, after a pause. "Remember, Charlotte, I can make anything fit. Just think of all the desserts I can fit in the car at once."

"You go get the rest of the milk crates in the hall," she said. "I'm going to put up some plates."

Then my mother rooted around for a hammer and some nails, and arranged her favorite plates on the walls. They were always porcelain, pink or green, with gold rims, and they brightened the sterile apartment, as she had hoped they would.

"There," she said, standing back and surveying the wall. "There. I'll put up the rest tomorrow."

We had stacks and stacks of plates in the milk crates, but my mother did, by the end of the week, hang each one on the wall.

And then, over time, even though we had so little room for the possessions we already had, my mother bought new items for the apartment. She *willed* it to be beautiful. White wrought-iron chairs scattered with blowsy cabbage roses. Robin's-egg blue porcelain cake stands, dotted with strawberries as small and red as lipstick kisses. Green-stemmed stools with speckled pink seats. She bought more than one of every item—often three or four—and when I asked her if we *needed* all this furniture, she said, "When you grow up, you can have plain white walls. Until then, *I* happen to care about style."

Besides, my mother said, we wouldn't stay here for long. She wanted to buy a house, if only she could ever save enough money.

My new Cambridge public elementary school was located about a five-minute walk from Harvard Square, where the Pudding was. It was also in walking distance of our new apartment. Every morning I got up and dealt with the usual drudgery that is the lot of any child in a school setting. Gym class was the worst. Not being athletic to begin with, I did not help matters by insisting on wearing dresses and patent leather Mary Janes to school. I spent recess sitting on a bench and reading novels, first romantic girls' books like *The Secret Garden* and *Anne of Green Gables*, and not long after that, things by the Brontës and Dickens and Henry James. Having spent so much time around grown-ups at the Pudding, I held in contempt things that were deemed age-appropriate. I never for a moment envied the lives of my

peers—lives of dodgeball, dioramas, "activities." I knew that
my life, by which I meant my life at the Pudding, existed on
an elevated plane.

I had only a couple of friends my own age, and I suppose
it didn't help that Benjamin—who was four years older than
I was—was always much more popular. And after my father
left the restaurant, Benjamin seemed to lose interest in it;
there were few people left in the kitchen whom he remembered. He no longer helped shell peas or roll pasta, and
within time he left the world of the Pudding for the world
of his peers, eating dinner there only on occasion. For me,
it would take years to leave the Pudding behind.

One of my mother's signature sayings was "Charlotte,
I am *not* the Entertainment Committee." She despised arts
and crafts, despised anything shoddy, lumpy, without style.
"Please," she begged me, "do not give me a pot holder for
Christmas." She would never have hung a drawing by me on
the wall when she could hang an exquisite antique botani-
cal print instead. She discouraged me from watching PG
and PG-13 movies, fearing that they would be wholesome
and feel-good, qualities she never held in high esteem.

I think it was around this time, when we moved to the
first of our dismal apartments, when I started to realize that
I only ever felt truly comfortable in the dining room of the
Pudding. If our new apartment was a temporary arrange-

ment, the Pudding, which had been there since I was born, was the only constant I had ever known, and it was only natural that it became my romance, my shimmering, sensuous center, the only place in which I was ever fully present. The rest of life was just waiting, waiting to go back to the Pudding. It was as if the lights were always *on* at the Pudding and *off* everywhere else.

But those lights were soft, and the gentle, impressionistic shadows they shed on the dining room were always in the most delicate palette of peach, rose, and pinkish cream.

Four

ANYTHING CAN ABSORB CHAMPAGNE

*I*n my bedroom at this time, there was a small round window, so high up I had to stand on a chair to reach it, that overlooked the building in which my parents, long ago in another era, another life, had met. It had been a restaurant called Peasant Stock, and they had both worked there. Like their marriage, though, Peasant Stock was no more.

What did my mother feel, I wondered, finding herself a divorced woman with two young children to support in the exact same neighborhood where, so many years before, she had fallen in love?

Sometimes at night, when my mother was still at the restaurant and I was home alone, I'd stare out of that window. I'd look down and try to imagine that building with my parents and their friends from when they were young. In my head, the scene at Peasant Stock was always a fine midsummer evening. Blue cheese and champagne grapes on a rustic cutting board, grappa flowing, everybody eating family-style. And my parents were still together.

It was my father I had to thank for these details—the grappa, the blue cheese, and so on—those tiny touches that could flicker a vanished world back to life in a child's imagination, for my father and never my mother used to tell me tales of Peasant Stock. My mother seldom spoke of the past, admonishing me once, "Charlotte, *I'm* getting to be the age where I ought to be thinking about the past. *You're* at the age where you ought to think a little more about the future."

Sometimes on summer evenings, my father would pick me up at the stoop in front of our apartment building and we would wander around the neighborhood, gazing at what remained of the haunts of my parents' youth. We always started at the Wine & Cheese Cask, a dusky, creaking-floored room where olives floated in fragrant buckets of oil, the men behind the counter smoked cigars, and, for a time, my mother had worked behind the counter slicing cheese. Then we went to Savenor's, the specialty food shop and butcher that delivered meat to all the fancy restaurants. Their most famous customer was Julia Child, who lived a couple of blocks away on Irving Street in the big gray Victorian, where she also filmed her television show.

My father told me, "I used to see her husband, Paul, all around the neighborhood. He always wore a black beret and these little wool shorts. Oh! He loved the pickles they used to have. Used to wrap them in wax paper and put them in this very small, very chic French string bag. I think this was when L'eggs panty hose had just come out, and we'd see him buying them for Julia at the corner drugstore."

At Savenor's, my father and I always got the same thing: roast beef and Boursin sandwiches with tomatoes on soft brown bread. All of the butchers who still worked there re- membered my father from back when he'd worked in the neighborhood. Sometimes they'd give us tours of the back room, beyond the cold-cuts counter. My father, an expert butcher himself, admired the pigs' knuckles and the ribbony cuts of skirt steak. "Cornish game hens!" he'd exclaim, stroking a fat-bellied golden bird on a string, a rapt look in his eyes. "Beautiful, beautiful."

Then we stopped at the ice truck, located next to Save- nor's in a bleak lot sprinkled with pebbles; for a dollar's worth of quarters, you could get a bag of ice twenty-four hours a day. No one was on hand operating the machine, but somehow it magically worked anyway. My father put the quarters in the slot and out clinked the bag of ice. As the sun set beyond the blue slate roofs of the neighborhood, we sucked on the ice cubes and I ran my hand over the hood of the ice truck, soft with shavings, dreaming of snow.

Here in this very lot on summer nights like this one, my

father said, the staff at Peasant Stock would sit on milk crates and swill warm red wine after close. Meanwhile, I sat on the edge of the curb, hugging my bare knees to my chest. I hoped that when I grew up I would find a place like Peasant Stock. I would stay up late and drink red wine and, like my parents, I would fall in love.

"I'm telling you, Char," my father said, ripping off the wrapper of his roast beef and Boursin sandwich, "if only we had some pickles. That's what makes one hell of a sandwich."

And then he described the pickles they used to sell at Savenor's in the old days. They came in a barrel. You had to reach in with a pair of blackened tongs to get them, and sometimes you had to reach pretty deep. They sold out right away, those pickles, that's how good they were. The best pickles in the whole world, my father said. And hearing this, I felt a faint pang of exclusion, because I'd never tasted those pickles. I'd been born too late for them and, it seemed, so many other wonderful things.

Being a bookish, solitary child, these stories of grown-ups—my parents' peers—made up the population in my head. Back when my parents were still together, there used to be a rather baroque-looking black sofa covered with cabbage roses in the living room of our farmhouse. It had passed from person to person at Peasant Stock before ending up with my parents. I once heard my mother remark, when she thought I wasn't listening, "Now *there's* a sofa that could tell you stories." And for a long time after that I was fascinated by that sofa, as though I, Charlotte, could will it to life to tell me these stories simply by gazing at it.

Once upon a time, my father told me, fine dining meant baked lobster and cocktails. Not all restaurants could be counted on to have wine lists. But at Peasant Stock, they made osso bucco and cassoulet, and for dessert things like macaroon soufflé with apricot-brandy sauce. They never served ice cream, plain ice cream, but some far more fascinating item called granita, in potent infusions of espresso or huckleberry or blood orange. And they always served fresh vegetables—this in the days, according to my father, when even the Ritz-Carlton served canned peas. Everything, everything was fresh.

"We used to call it Caesar's Palace," my father said of Peasant Stock. "That's because every time someone ordered a Caesar salad, we'd coddle the egg for the dressing right then and there. Our fingers were always eggy, and they ached a hell of a lot, too."

My mother, who baked the desserts, used Blue Mountain coffee in the coffee-flavored granita. It was spectacularly expensive, but food costs did not much enter into the equation. *Food costs* was, for that matter, perhaps not even a term people had started to use. This was long before restaurants had consultants and chefs were celebrities. I'd heard her say, "Peasant Stock was the first place I ever tasted grappa." The very word *grappa*, in my mother's voice, seemed to signify sensuality, pleasure, discovery—happiness itself. Through the years, she would order it off and on, whenever she wanted to feel festive. I recall her once saying to me about Peasant Stock, "The cheeses were always so *soft*," as though all cheeses since had hardened for her, spoiled.

Peasant Stock was a truly democratic place, where everyone shared the chores; my father recalled Harvard professors wandering into the kitchen and drying dishes for an evening. It was the kind of place, my father went on, "where everyone had a PhD and drove a cab on the side. Oh! That reminds me. Remember Alyce? *She* used to drive a cab, back in the day." Alyce had worked, briefly, behind the line at the Pudding in my father's time, and was a rather curious figure in a kitchen, being for one thing an older woman and for another a well-educated Southern belle, via New Orleans and Radcliffe. In honor of her birthday, my father used to cook her a grand Southern meal, featuring turtle soup, creamed oysters, and strawberry layer cake.

"She did?" I exclaimed, unable to picture this fine-boned woman who I always thought of as wearing long, swishy Marimekko dresses sitting behind the wheel of a taxi. Alyce had always taken an interest in me, and when she and her husband, Philip, used to come visit our farmhouse, she always brought me the most luxurious picture books.

"Oh, yeah, just to make a buck. I think maybe it was just something for her to do between marriages. Anyway, it was the seventies! Things were different then. You know she had an affair with Updike? She was at Radcliffe the same time he was at Harvard. She was always talking about him. Updike, Updike, Updike. I used to get sick of the name!"

"Oh my God," I said, "so that explains it. The last time I saw her"—she and Philip had come in for dinner at the Pudding—"she was asking me what I was reading these days, and had I read Updike yet? There was this look in her eyes when she said the name."

"Yup," said my father, and laughed. And I, filling in the pieces of the narrative, marveled at the succulence of detail, the beautiful banquet of grown-up life. I couldn't wait till I grew up and worked at someplace like Peasant Stock myself.

"Actually, between you and me, Char, Philip used to kind of drive the staff nuts. His big thing was collecting old stamps and rare coins. Coins and stamps! Fucking kill me already." My father rolled his eyes. "You know me, Char, I can be interested in almost anything, but not *that* crap. He used to come into Peasant Stock and go through the register *looking for coins*. And there we were, like, trying to run a restaurant! Getting the food out of the kitchen and feeding the customers and everything. We used to call him 'Stamps' sometimes behind his back."

My father and I walked and walked down Kirkland Street, the sun beginning to set. Even in summertime, the light slanting down was a thin, dim yellow, not a rich, happy yellow. Cambridge was a melancholy town. Its color palette was faded. We passed Sanders Theatre, a looming, fairy-tale structure that seemed to belong more to England than anywhere in America. And right across from Sanders Theatre was Sparks House, home of the Reverend Peter J. Gomes, longtime minister of the Memorial Church and one of the well-known local characters. Everybody could see him coming, a rotund yet suave figure turned out with dandyish precision in elaborate three-piece suits. His watch fob—always seen hanging from his breast pocket—seemed to my child's eye like some magical toy, which, if you tugged its long golden chain, might rocket you, *Alice in Wonderland*–style, to another kingdom. Reverend Gomes often ate at the Pudding, and every spring my mother and Mary-Catherine went to the lavish garden party he held on the lawn of Sparks House, lilacs wildly feathering the hedges that kept the prying eyes of strangers out. In season—but only *in season*, he stressed—he wore a straw boater hat. That hat signified the turning of the season in Cambridge the same way the lilacs did: a hopeful emblem of balmy weather.

"Oh, Peter Gomes!" exclaimed my father. "That guy. You know who works for him?" My father named the former owner of Peasant Stock. "I think he does catering for him. Christ! I don't think I'd wish the likes of *catering for Peter Gomes* on my worst enemy. Imagine it: tea parties for Harvard choirboys and all that WASP-y crap. I bet you'd have to serve tea sandwiches!" My father shook his head. He didn't care for tea sandwiches, or for miniature food generally. He was from Chicago; he liked a hot dog with all the fixings, a Reuben with plenty of Russian dressing, the works.

By then we were also near Julia Child's house, just a couple of blocks down Irving Street. I often passed her in the mornings on my walk to school. You couldn't miss her; she was so tall! I asked my father, "Did Julia Child ever come in to Peasant Stock?"

"One night, there I was, making stuffing," my father recalled. "Corn bread stuffing with oysters and bacon. You know the one, Char. Your mother still makes it. Anyway, in comes Julia, you can't miss her, that height, that voice, and I'm just making my stuffing and then I look over at her as she's trying to open a champagne bottle with the side of a cleaver—that's an old kitchen trick. And then *pop!* The champagne spills all over my stuffing. Julia turns to me and says, " 'Now, now. Don't you worry. *Anything* can absorb champagne.' "

Anything can absorb champagne—not bad words to live by, I think, and words that my mother and Mary-Catherine, taking over the Pudding after my father left, certainly took to heart. For they continued to run the restaurant in the shadow of Julia Child's effusive spirit, wanting dining there to be like going to a friend's fabulous dinner party every night.

*M*y father had been living with someone else— someone else from the Peasant Stock crowd— when he fell in love with my mother. The feeling, apparently, was mutual, for my mother also was living with someone else at the time, and immediately left him to be with my father.

I heard that my father walked out on the other woman one afternoon, wordlessly and quite without warning, while she was standing at the kitchen counter chopping carrot sticks. The only thing he bothered to take with him was the English sheepdog, Benjy, who went on to live with my parents and was still around in my earliest childhood, before he died, run over by a snow tractor on Dudley Road.

I have only heard tell of the incident of the carrot sticks and have only the vaguest memories of the bloody chaos surrounding Benjy's death, so all of this is only speculation on my part; all of it relies on my imagination, the same thing I use to summon up the soft cheeses, the granitas, at Peasant Stock. Was there a warning in the event in this other woman's kitchen of just how easily my father could pick up and leave? This scene—simple, elegant, and darkly comic—expressed a great deal about my father's understated style: no explanations, no regrets. As did the fact that he took none of his possessions with him (not for nothing did I often hear people refer to my father as "the last of the bohemians"—this was years, years after other people from Peasant Stock had gone on to make money and buy fancy real estate, leaving the lifestyle, if not, they supposed, the values of the sixties behind them). And then there was his bothering to take the dog: also a foreshadowing of events to come, because my father was fond of animals and had a weakness for collecting them, although a number of their lives ended, like Benjy's, in macabre deaths.

My mother was already pregnant with Benjamin when my parents were married in a simple ceremony befitting that less materialistic time. They spent their honeymoon in Vermont, a conventional enough choice, I suppose, except that for some reason Mary-Catherine went along with them. In fact, Mary-Catherine met my father before my mother did, and, compelled by his moody, cerebral magnetism, had even had a crush on him. No matter. It was my understanding, even as a child, that Peasant Stock had abounded in many love triangles far less innocent than this one, which went on to fuse friendship and business. And many years later, when I was all grown up and my father was dead, too young, of his third and final heart attack, my mother and I sat down to a breakfast of English muffins and blueberry preserves at a fancy resort in Woodstock, Vermont, on a radiant midsummer morning. My mother sighed and mentioned coming to Vermont for her honeymoon; an unusual nostalgic detour for her, for she still doesn't talk that much of the past. Then she said, "Mary-Catherine Deibel came with us on our honeymoon, did I ever tell you that?" My mother laughed. Then, surveying the wreckage—but also the delicious richness—of her life: "Oh, well. I guess I always figured I'd end up with one or the other of them. And so I did."

As for Peasant Stock, it served its last glass of grappa in 1987, when I was six years old and, incidentally, just around the time my parents' marriage was cracking up on Dudley Road.

There were certain foods that my mother claimed she

could no longer bear to eat, years and then even decades after she had worked at Peasant Stock, because, she would explain, she had eaten too much of them back in the day.

These forbidden foods included Mary-Catherine's famous chicken liver pâté, which had been served flecked with chives in a deep, cut-glass bowl along with buttered toast points at untold numbers of parties in Cambridge, and which, potent with criminal quantities of butter, sherry, and heavy cream, was to me one of the most decadent foods in the entire world. But my mother could no longer eat that pâté, or anything at all with the herb tarragon. Nor could she eat certain game meats, for Peasant Stock used to sometimes host spectacular eight-course game-meat dinners over which my father, who loved such meats, presided. I still have a yellowed menu from one of these dinners; the year was 1976, and my father was serving Wild European Boar with Apples and Sage and Hare Flamed in Chartreuse.

And something about my mother's expressions when she reacted to these foods (the tone of voice she used when saying the word *tarragon*, for instance, unlike the word *grappa*), the way she flinched away from even the possibility of tasting them again, told me something, even when I was just a child, about the vague, bitter under-taste of the Peasant Stock romance, of the hippie era itself. Maybe, even, of love,

from the point of view of a woman; that it contained a mul-
titude of flavors and that some of these you might, years
later, seek to reclaim. *Grappa.* Some you wished you might
erase from your memory forever. *Tarragon.* These were the
overlapping tastes—the adult consequences—of love.

Five

THE LAVENDER
BLONDE

Whenever people found out that my mother owned the Pudding, the first question inevitably would be "Which one is your mother? The one with the sunglasses?" For sunglasses were my mother's trademark; never did she appear in public, day or night, without them. Men were forever going up to her on the street and gushing, "Honey, I *love* the glasses." Enormous Chanel frames swept movie star–style across her face, their lenses tinted a custom-made shade of purple-blue and casting soft lavender shadows across her face. When she was younger, my mother was told she looked like the actress Kim Novak, the Lavender Blonde. On the rare occasions when she took off her sunglasses, you could see that my mother's face was delicate and kittenish; her eyes were silvery green. But you almost never saw them.

"I've got to get my waist back," my mother had said not

long after my father left, and to her credit, that's exactly what she did. She achieved this by exercising extraordinary discipline in the face of constant exposure to fattening food. At the restaurant, she stirred vats of roasted-sweet-red-pepper soup and frosted triple-layer coconut cakes, working in the kitchen for up to twelve hours a day. Sometimes she swiped a sliver of prosciutto off the butcher block or ordered a Caesar salad for lunch, but she hardly ever snacked in the kitchen. Her logic was simple: "Either you love wonderful food or wonderful clothes," she told me. "I happen to love wonderful clothes more."

Her waist, she told me, was now twenty-six inches. Over time, it got to be twenty-five and twenty-four. I did not know how many inches women's waists were supposed to be, but my mother's waist *did* look small, especially when she suctioned it into cinch belts. The belts were black patent leather or crocodile; they had gold and rhinestone buckles and interlocking Chanel Cs and sometimes fringe. "The thicker the belt, the tinier the waist," she said.

Every night, my mother came home to dress up before going back into the restaurant again. She looked a wreck from the long hours in the kitchen: hair sliding out of tortoise-shell combs, pink lipstick smeared from taste-testing, apron splattered with bacon grease and chocolate ganache.

"Oh, God, what time is it?" she would say. "Charlotte, run the bathtub. They're expecting me in forty minutes."

I ran the tub and filled it with the waxy lavender petals we kept in a glass jar on the sink. And when she stepped back out of the bathroom, it was as if all the sweat of the kitchen had oozed down the drain. My mother's skin always smelled delicious; her arms felt as smooth as mine. She slid her legs into Velvet De Luxe Wolford panty hose and fastened the clasp of one of her black lace bras with the shirring around the cups. I had heard her say that wearing nice underwear was the only way a woman in a kitchen could still feel like a woman.

My mother always wore Joy perfume, which at one time had been the most expensive perfume in the world. Its exuberant femininity, no expense spared, suited my mother's brand of excess, containing thousands of jasmine petals and twenty-eight May roses per ounce. I watched her as she untwisted the gold-capped square bottle and dabbed the scent behind her temples. Instantly it perfumed the apartment, blotting out the lavender fragrance from her bath.

"Wear this, Mummy," I said, sifting through the finery to extract a jacket or shell for her to wear on top.

"Charlotte, you don't understand," she said. "It needs to *nip* in." She gestured to her waist strapped underneath the ribbon piping of her bouffant skirt. "What I look good in is a top—well, a beautiful fitted cashmere sweater—that stops at the waist, and then a full skirt. But midcalf—never too long and *never, never short.*"

It was true. My mother did not show her legs, only her waist, only her breasts in sweetheart necklines of cocktail dresses or off-the-shoulder cashmere sweaters. Her legs were short, and despite all the weight she'd lost, they looked pretty much the same as before; they would never be slender. But the flash of silk stockings under rustling skirts looked like a naughty promise, as though she had hidden the rest of her legs to provoke the viewers' fantasies—really they stretched on forever.

"Remember the waist," she told me, spraying gusts of Joy perfume in the air. "Remember the waist and the legs don't matter."

Then, after she had wrapped herself in an evening cape and found her keys, she swept out the door, leaving a trail of debris, like the scene of a movie queen's murder: an overturned gilded mirror, lurid smudges of pink lipstick, the inky spill of an open mascara tube. (Sometimes I picked up the belts she had littered the floor with and tried to fasten them around my midriff. As I got older, and rather chubby for a time, my baby fat would dribble over the buckle. Of course, I thought to myself, my mother's belts didn't fit me—they only fit *her*.)

At the same time my mother got thin, she threw out all her shoes and replaced them with high heels, which she now wore every day. The other grown-up women I knew owned black stilettos or navy or camel-colored pumps. But my mother bought zebra-print T-straps and jeweled black satin evening boots, watermelon-pink mules with matching polish peeking out of the open toes and stacked Lucite slippers, heels with feathers, heels with ribbons lacing ballerina-style up the ankles.

My mother did everything in these shoes; she even cooked in them sometimes. Her heels dug into the cut-out holes of the rubber mats behind the stoves as she swept through the grease and flames and grunting men, and I never saw her slip. She kept extra pairs around the restaurant— spiked heels stuck out of cubbyholes in the office, and shoe boxes piled up on top of the walk-in refrigerator in the kitchen. "The right shoes," she told me. "That's all I'll ever need: the right shoes and a trusty exterminator." She could wear her apron in the dining room, she said, but nobody would care, as long as her high heels caught the sparkle from the chandeliers. *And* they lengthened her legs.

"Leopard," my mother used to say, "is my favorite neutral."

She liked the way it went with other things: emerald, camel, salmon, dusty gold. The off-kilter exuberance of leopard and plaid colliding was a favorite visual motif of hers both in interior design and dress. She would place a leopard cushion against a plaid silk armchair, or wear round-toed leopard pumps with little plaid socks and black palazzo—or what I always thought of as "hostess"—pants.

Her signature piece of clothing was a leopard-print swing coat, Italian, with wide bell-shaped sleeves and a lining of mocha velveteen. This she wore for years and years. Animal-like, it marked her territory. If you walked into the restaurant and saw it slung over one of the backs of the red velvet chairs, you knew my mother was there.

One afternoon not long after we had moved to Cambridge, I ran into one of the restaurant's deliverymen on Mass Ave. He smiled at me, but I didn't smile back. I thought that if I smiled at him he might talk to me, and I didn't remember his name. My mother said it was rude to say hello without adding the person's name at the end, and so I kept on walking.

"I am so disappointed in you," my mother told me later that week. "Jim, our fruit supply man, stopped by today and he said you didn't smile at him when you saw him on the street. What is this? Anybody would think you were shy."

It was bad manners to forget his name and bad manners not to smile, bad manners to speak to him and bad manners to ignore him. Bad manners, everywhere.

If I forgot a name in the dining room, I thought all conversation would halt, as when a busboy dropped a tray of martini glasses and they shattered against the linoleum floor of the kitchen. Or as when the waiters brushed against the light switch and for a few moments the customers could see the dust bunnies in the rafters and the runs in the curtains. All would be revealed, and I would disgrace us both.

"You're either on or you're off," my mother liked to say. "You either stay home or you go out and you pull yourself together." I could tell when she was off and when she was on from the tone of her voice. It changed all the time. In the front room, it sounded as thickly sweet as the Joy perfume she rubbed on her wrists, and it oozed over the tables. *"Hello,"* she said, greeting people. She rolled the word off her tongue and dabbed traces of lipstick on strangers' cheeks.

When she went into the kitchen, her voice dropped several octaves. It was bold, like the sound of her stilettos striking the linoleum. "That trout looks as soft as rice pudding," she said. "This is *not* an old person's home." Then she swept into the dining room, and her heels went soft against the velvet carpet, and her voice went soft again. *"Hello. Hello. Hello."*

So when the waiters came up to my table, pen and paper in hand, I knew what to do. I raised my voice, not loud but high. The voice wound up inside me, somewhere underneath my party dresses, and surged to the top, as when I twisted off the cap to a bottle of grenadine and it produced a squeak and then sweetness. Every thank-you was like another shot of the syrup, straight, but the waiters didn't mind. They told my mother I was a lovely child. I had lovely manners.

There was another rule about manners; my mother said it was the most important one of all, never, never, under any circumstances, to be broken.

"No crying at the restaurant, Charlotte. Remember, it's a public place."

Six

NOT IN FRONT
OF THE
CUSTOMERS

*O*ne night when I crawled underneath the bar to take a nap, I noticed that it seemed smaller. When I stretched my legs out, my Mary Janes dangled out from the flap of the tablecloth, and I imagined that if one of the customers saw them, they would think they belonged to a corpse. I rather liked that thought. It was so *dramatic*. Trying to make myself comfortable, I drew my knees together; I leaned onto my side; I tried to rearrange the bundles of linen. Nothing helped. The air smelled starchy, as it always did underneath the bar, but the scent bothered me now, and I coughed from all the dust.

Thud. I had slammed my head against the oak tabletop. I worried that the glasses above would rattle and shake, but I heard nothing, only a dull drumming in my ears. The pink bow on top of my headband was crushed. And for the rest of the night, even after I had wiggled out from underneath the bar, I felt dizzy; the gold threads in the carpet looked fuzzier, the lights in the chandeliers dimmer.

That was the first of the kingdoms from which I would be exiled—the kingdom underneath the bar.

Forever after that, I had no relief from the dining room. There was no place to hide. I had to adapt to it, however I could.

Weekends were hard. Weekends my mother had no time for me. So on Saturday afternoons, I used to pace around Harvard Square, looking for something to do. I went to the Coop, where wind blew into the main room with the marble floors and it seemed to me they sold only black kneesocks, fountain pens that leaked or had run out of ink, postcards that had peeled at the sides, and chocolate Easter eggs left on the shelves in all seasons in battered pink or red boxes. I went to Café Pamplona, the underground coffee shop on Bow Street, where the waiters were looming and grumpy, the parfait spoons rusty, and the menu—gazpacho, swampy green and slithering with onions, and a pork and pickle sandwich on a fried bun—never changed. There was also Colonial Drug, the old-fashioned perfume store with the leopard hatboxes and a velvet carpet the color of a crushed blackberry, and Cardullo's, the specialty food shop, also with a velvet rug, which sold hand-painted tins of caviar and beribboned bags of chocolate almonds that looked like they had been there since the 1950s. And the Brattle Theatre: it showed *Casablanca* every Valentine's Day and film noir on Monday nights, yellowed fluff peeked through the Prussian-blue leather seats, and the clock on the wall had been broken for as long as I could remember.

Then came Saturday night. When I was growing up, Saturday night was the big event of the week. It was the grand crescendo toward which all the week's activities had built. *Saturday night*—the words alone had a glamour and a menace about them. *Saturday night!* One hundred and fifty customers, two hundred, three hundred, four hundred. *Saturday night!* "No main course for you tonight," my mother would tell me. "Maybe an appetizer if you order early." *Saturday night!* "Here, help out, why don't you? Polish some silver; light the candles; fold a napkin into a tiny pink swan. But, don't forget the customers. Customers are coming!"

My main job on Saturday nights was to stay out of the way of the customers. And then sometimes I did little errands or chores. Like sometimes on summer nights when the chefs were wilting behind the line in that smoldering Victorian kitchen, where the heat was not even relieved by ceiling fans, they would send me to go get beers from behind the bar. I loved doing that. I would plunge my hands into the ice bucket, basking in the cold, until one of the bartenders pushed me out of the way. Then I would stumble back into the kitchen.

"Thanks, kiddo," said Carla, standing at the head of the line. When she banged a butcher knife against the bottle top, the top flew up in the air; I hoped it hadn't landed in the tins of prep garnishes. But Carla didn't bother to look; she just lit another cigarette.

"Don't make yourself too comfortable, kiddo," she said. "I'll need another beer soon."

What was she talking about? *Nobody* could be too comfortable in a kitchen. There was no place to sit. Oh, for the days when I could crawl underneath the bar and get away from it all! Now there was no place for me, and especially on Saturday nights. Saturday nights were *the worst.*

"Here, kiddo."

Carla always called me *kiddo*, not *sweetie* or *honey* like the waiters did. She scraped a piece of tenderloin off the pan and flicked it onto a brown paper towel. The meat reddened the paper.

"That's for you."

On Saturday nights, I didn't order dinner. Instead, I ate whatever snippets the chefs doled out to me: lopsided zucchini blossoms or clams casino swiped off private-party platters. There were always plenty of samples of food to eat in the kitchen, and chefs love feeding people. Carla used to save the most rare meat for me. She knew I liked it—one of my favorite foods was steak tartare on buttered toast points—and the customers would have sent back meat as rare as this tenderloin.

"Thank you, Carla," I said.

"You and your *thank-you*s—would you give it up? I'm not one of those pansies in the front room who's just dying to freshen your . . . your . . . What are those things called?"

"Shirley Temples?"

"Yeah, yeah, those."

I picked the piece of tenderloin off the paper towel. In the front room, I had good table manners, but you couldn't feel graceful if you had no knife or fork. I hoped the juice wouldn't splatter my new party dress, a garden-party dress: white muslin printed with cabbage roses and a white petticoat underneath that puffed out like one of the meringues on the trays in the cold station. It also had a trailing rose-chiffon sash that reminded me of my mother's cocktail dresses with the small waists; I loved that sash the most.

"Here." She handed me another napkin; the tenderloin had stained my fingertips red. "I know how you hate to be messy."

I wondered when we would go home. It must have been eight o'clock now, rush time. Customers' conversation roared through the doors, and I heard my mother's voice, her kitchen voice. "Buck up!" she told the waiters. "Can't you see the kitchen's in the weeds?" I supposed she was out on the floor now, fluttering from table to table, planting Coco Pink kisses on cheek after cheek, and swerving away on the tips of the stilettos.

"Watch out!" said Carla. I looked and saw flames spouting off the stove. "Go . . . go somewhere."

I pranced off the rubber mat onto the bare floor between the rows of the stoves and the pastry station. My patent leather Mary Janes slid on a sprig of buttered parsley. Meanwhile, the waiters charged down the aisle and grabbed the desserts waiting on the top of the shelf.

"Where's the lemon budino for C-3?" one of them asked. "Hurry it up, they're the table from hell . . ."

I hid in the cold room. I yanked open the steel door and stepped up to the sawdust floor. The gust of air from the freezer prickled my bare legs underneath the petticoat. I stood very still in the center of the cold room. If I moved, I thought one of the Cornish game hens swinging from the ceiling might fall off its string.

"Coming through," said Charlie, opening the door. He was lugging a crate full of lobsters for the lobster salad entree my mother put on the menu every summer. "Well, hello, Miss Charlotte."

Charlie was one of the black guys my mother had hired from the homeless shelter in downtown Boston. He was from Tennessee, and my mother chose him because of what she called "his Southern charm" and because the day she went to the homeless shelter he was wearing a three-piece violet polyester suit and saddle shoes he still bothered to polish.

"That's one sweet dress you've got on, Miss Charlotte," he said. "Now do you mind if I get through here?"

"Sorry, Charlie."

I dashed out of the cold room. I found myself in front of the line: flames leapt, chefs huffed, waiters whizzed. Their voices all blended together.

"Two ducks. Three Caesars. One beef Wellington, hold the foie gras."

"We can't hold the foie gras," Carla said. "Do these people even know what beef Wellington is? It's *inside* the puff pastry."

"I told them, I told them, but—"

More orders, more voices: "Three arugulas," they said. "Two crab vicars, one gnocchi, one truffle tagliatelle—no, one truffle risotto, sorry."

They clipped the orders on the metal shelf in front of the

stoves. When the orders fell from the grip of the shelf, I dipped down to pick them up from the floor. Nobody remembered to say thank you. Nobody called me *honey* or *sweetheart*, either, as they did in the front room, because nobody had the time.

The double doors swung back and forth, the chain jangling between them. Champagne buckets skidded across the floor. Wine corks stuck straight ahead in the air like daggers. Red-pepper soup dribbled off the edges of the bowls and onto the floor. The flames of the chefs' cigarettes danced above the flames of the stoves.

"Coming through!" the waiters announced. "Coming through!"

I ducked underneath the white linen sleeves and porcelain plates above me and scurried past the cold room and the stoves until I reached the pastry station. It must have been somebody's birthday, because Sarah, the pastry chef, was standing next to the Cuisinart on the floor and lighting candles on a slice of coconut layer cake. We had always been friends, Sarah and I, but tonight she didn't even bother to say hello to me.

Whoosh! What was happening? I spun around and around as puffs of whipped cream tickled my face and splattered my curls like snowflakes in a blizzard. This was it: I was becoming a charlotte au chocolat, just like people used to tease me. *One of these nights when we run out of charlottes, we're going to plop you on a plate and top you in whipped cream . . .* Maybe everyone on the staff was in on the plan. First they were smothering me in whipped cream, and then—

A blade. I must have been standing too close and my dress got caught on the machine. A blade, whirling toward my waist. It was the blade of the Cuisinart: something had caught on the Cuisinart.

Then I heard the sound of shredding fabric. The Cuisinart stopped and I toppled backward onto the floor.

"Damn it," Sarah said. She blew out the candles and slapped the matches down on the table. "Why doesn't this thing ever just work?" She peered into the bowl of the Cuisinart and reached in with her fingers. "*This* is a new one."

She held what looked like two stubby, frayed pink ribbons in her hands. My sash! The blade had severed my sash in half. I stood up from the ground. My dress hung limp around my waist.

"My sash," I said, spreading my fingertips toward Sarah. But it was too late. She had flicked it in the garbage. "My sash . . ."

"Oh, that was yours!" she said. "God, Char, I'm sorry. I didn't even think about it. Do you know, last week your mother said she would give a raise to the person who found—" She turned the Cuisinart on again. "To the person who found her ring. That really big pink plastic Chanel one. We think it got into the bouillabaisse . . ."

One of the waiters stormed into the pastry station. "Sarah, what the hell happened to that budino?"

"Sorry, sorry . . ."

"Spare me the apology till you see my tip."

He walked away. Sarah reached for the container marked LEMON BUDINO in Magic Marker, took one of the long wooden spoons, and scooped the pale yellow cream onto a plate. "Could you pass me the raspberries?" she asked me. "They're under the table. God, does this feel like the longest night or what?"

I handed her the box of raspberries. "Do you know what time it is?"

"Around nine, I think."

Nine! We didn't leave on Saturdays until midnight at the earliest. I sighed.

"Thanks, Sarah."

But Sarah wasn't there; she had already sped off some-where. I peeked into the garbage and saw, mixed in with pulpy strawberries and paper towels streaked with olive oil, just a sliver of rose chiffon.

*M*y mother was tough about most things but had one great phobia, which she passed down to me: rodents. In those days, Harvard Square was dirtier than it is today, and the T station had recently undergone a major construction job. For a number of years, there was a big hole in the middle of the Square, increasing the sheer number of rodents as well as the insouciance with which they roamed the streets. You often saw them lurking on the edges of Dumpsters or slithering down alleys.

The Pudding, being located in a ramshackle Victorian building, had rodents in the basement. Almost no one ever went there, but people who had came back, as if from beyond the grave, with warnings: *Charlotte, whatever you do, don't ever go down to the basement!*

But one night I happened to spot a mouse *upstairs*, behind the bar. Instinctively, I screamed. "A mouse!" I wailed. "A mouse! Mummy, there's a—"

My mother swooped down and cupped my mouth with her hand. When she spoke, it was in a whisper. "Don't say that. Don't ever say that again. *Not in front of the customers!*"

She gripped my hand and we walked across the dining room toward the office. There were no mice in the office.

They only existed in the kitchen, or behind the bar, or in the bathroom, and especially in the alley, skirting around the edges of the Dumpster. At least the one I had just seen was dead, caught in the crack of the ice-cream chest.

"It wasn't big enough to be the *other* thing," I said as soon as my mother closed the door to the office. "But it was dirty, and I saw the little pink . . ."

She was shaking, as she always did whenever anyone mentioned rodents.

"And it was *dead*. It—"

We heard a knock on the door. It was Sarah.

"Deborah, I wanted to know if you had ordered any more strawberries for— Hey, Char, what's the matter?"

I paused.

"A mouse," my mother said. "And once I saw one in the cold station."

"Oh, the *cold station*," Sarah said, eyeing my mother. "Well, you know what I bet that was? That wasn't any mouse. That was just a piece of my new fur coat; it must have fallen off."

"It shed," my mother said after a pause. "That happens with furs."

I pictured the object I had seen in the crack of the ice-cream chest. It was gray and fuzzy. I pictured fur coats. They were gray and fuzzy, too. It couldn't have been a mouse I saw in the ice-cream chest, after all.

But I still saw mice around the restaurant, dead and alive. A fat one bobbed in a ring of filthy soapsuds in a yellow bucket on the floor of the kitchen bathroom. Pink tails waggled and spun behind the stoves. Everywhere, even in the dining room, I looked for clumps of gray and flashes of moist pink. The rodents were winning: the exterminator told my mother that there was no hope for a nineteenth-century building two blocks away from the subway station. "Please give me a nice, romantic table for two," he told her when he and his wife came in to dinner for their anniversary. "Not too close to the bait stations."

And the rats; rats invaded the kitchen stairs. I knew it. They gorged on bacon scraps and buttered endive leaves, wriggled in and out of holes shielded with spiderwebs, and then waddled back to the parking lot. Sometimes, at the end of the night, my mother and I saw them slinking down the alley as we approached the car. Their thick tails twitched and their eyes glinted. They surveyed my mother and me, wrapped in our finery, coolly.

"Mummy! A rat! A rat!"

"Charlotte! A rat! A—"

Then we shrieked. We, who never cried in the dining room, shrieked all the way down Holyoke Street. We ran all the way to the cabstand outside of Out of Town News, and my mother did not go anywhere near the alley and our car until the next morning, when the rats were curled up underneath the Dumpsters, coiled in the gathering shadows, asleep.

There was a night when I must have been no more than seven or eight years old when my mother and I were driving through Harvard Square. This was at the end of the kind of deathless summer evening where the chefs, slaving behind the line in that ramshackle Victorian kitchen, rich with prosciutto, fried sage, ricotta, and sweating, salted half-moons of cantaloupe, used to beg me to go get them bottles of beer from the bar. After locking up the restaurant, my mother and I made it safely through the alley, dodging the rats as usual. We got in the car; we started to drive through the Square. Street musicians were still playing, even if, by now, only the homeless people were listening. And then my eyes landed on a couple making love, standing up, right in the middle of Mass Ave, in front of one of the gates of Harvard Yard, with most of their clothes still on. The man, with great, nearly angelic tenderness, was undoing the buttons of the woman's white linen blouse. I looked and looked; my mother didn't say a word. Then we drove on until the couple, and Harvard Square itself, receded from view.

Although, in my life as a woman, I was to go on and find at least a couple of men who touched me that same way—with that same angelic gaze in the eyes—and although I did have moments of pleasure that made me recapture, almost, the divine ache of letting beads of clementine ice dissolve on my child's tongue at the Pudding, there was never anything to compare to the feeling of pure, buoyant sensation, of the limitless abundance of the physical world, I experienced that night. No, there was never again to be a moment approaching the splendor and mystery of that one, of the sight of those two strangers making love, as naturally and as full of innocent sensual life as those cantaloupes or those gentle, scalloped slopes of ricotta in wax paper.

And what of the rats? What has become of them? I suppose that if their offspring are no longer in that parking lot, by now they have gone on to other Dumpsters, other neighborhoods, being resourceful rats, and from one generation to another, long for this world.

Seven

CERISE DELIGHT

*F*or a long time, I used to go behind the bar and hoard the small glass jars of maraschino cherries. I'd twist off the red tops and flick the stems in a pile, like the red ribbons of opened Christmas presents. Afterward, I licked the perfumed liquid off my fingertips and reached for another jar. Adults didn't like maraschino cherries; nobody ate them but me. "Never give Charlotte just one cherry in her Shirley Temple," everybody said. "Make it at least five or six." But I tired of cherries, just cherries.

So after a time, lemon, lime, and orange twists snaked around the brims. Dollops of Chantilly cream floated like water lilies on top of mint leaves in the fizzy pink water. The bartenders dipped sugar swizzles in grenadine overnight so they would look like pink rhinestones, capped cocktail straws with berries they had rolled in honey, and looped lemon peels around the stems of martini glasses. Everyone on the staff called those ones "Bondage Shirley Temples," and then they would wink at one another.

The customers stared at my drinks as they passed through the dining room perched on the waiters' trays like brightly plumed birds. Sometimes they pulled members of the staff aside and asked, "*What* is that child drinking?" Other times they pointed to my table and told the waiters they would have the same drink as I was having, whatever it was. But they did not get Chantilly cream and lemon peels, and only got the proper amount of maraschino cherries. After all, they were grown-ups.

Everybody used to drink out in the open in the dining room; it was no big deal. My friends the waiters Henry and Alex used to drink something called Brandy Alexanders, which were pale, creamy brown, like the brown of some beautiful mushroom, and went down like milk shakes. I knew this because sometimes they let me have a sip of them, and they tasted divine.

"Like chocolate milk," said Henry, jangling his brandy snifter with a slim, expressive wrist. "Right, sweetheart?"

Henry and Alex hardly ever called me Charlotte. They called me *sweetheart* or *honey* or *movie star*, or simply, *love*.

Sometimes they called me Cordelia, after Sebastian's youngest sister in *Brideshead Revisited*. This was the eighties; the miniseries had recently been on television and all things *Brideshead* were the rage. Henry and Alex were around the year I went trick-or-treating as Cordelia in stiff, rust-colored taffeta. Sometimes during setup in the dining room—polishing glasses, folding napkins into tiny pink swans—we acted out Cordelia's grand monologue, the one beginning "Sebastian's drunk!" We practiced our best British accents, and the fact that *Brideshead Revisited* was a book about alcoholism quite escaped me.

Henry and Alex said they would take me for the whole afternoon some Saturday; I loved it when people on the staff did things with me outside of the restaurant. They wanted to take me back-to-school shopping at the Neiman Marcus children's department, and afterward we could have a sleepover at their apartment, which had, they said, a lavender bedroom. Lavender was my favorite color, second only to pink.

I couldn't wait for my day with Henry and Alex. They said we could rent old movies and eat cucumber tea sandwiches off heart-shaped plates. I could even use Henry's Chanel face cream. Henry had such smooth skin that my mother had begged him to tell her what product he used. "Why do you think I wait tables?" he said. "So I can afford Chanel." After that, my mother used Chanel face cream, too, then the tanning lotion. "Where did you get that tan?" people asked her. "The Chanel counter," she said.

One time Henry and Alex picked me up after school. We were going to bake a fruitcake for the staff Christmas party that was coming up, and so they took me to their apartment with the lavender walls and the fluffy white rug on the living-room floor. Henry made me a cream cheese and olive sandwich, and Alex took a glass bottle of chocolate milk out of the refrigerator. "Just for you," he said. I checked to see if they wanted any of the chocolate milk before I poured myself another glass, but Alex was already mixing gin and tonic water and Henry was squeezing the limes, so I finished off the bottle.

"What do we need for the fruitcake?" I asked. I feared they took a long time to make. My mother had baked them at the farmhouse; she used to let me lick the brown sugar and bourbon off the sheets of wax paper she had spread on top to help them cool.

"God," said Alex. "I don't know. Flour?"

"No flour," Henry said, opening the cupboard. It was empty.

"Eggs," I said. "You always need eggs. And then fruit. Currants and—"

Henry jerked open the door to the refrigerator. I saw only the carton of cream cheese, and bottles, and bottles.

"How about sherry?" I said, wondering where they kept their cookbooks. "Sherry, or bourbon?"

"Oh," they said together, "we have *those*."

I was about to ask for a pen to make a shopping list when Henry said, "*Flour*. Who wants to bring a lumpy old bag of that stuff into the home, anyway? I'll tell you what: let's just open the sherry. Want another sandwich, sweetie?"

That Christmas party there was no fruitcake, as it happened, and Henry and Alex didn't come to the party at all. I waited for them by the banister, scraping the gold-leaf garnish off a pinecone with my fingertips. After an hour I began to climb the stairs to the dining room. The pinecone lay split open on the foot of the stairs and slits of gold leaf gleamed against the dark carpet.

I never did see Henry and Alex again, though I heard tell that they'd moved to San Francisco.

After Henry and Alex left, I became friends with a new waitress named McKenzie. McKenzie was even blonder than my mother, and almost as glamorous. Her hair was bobbed and her lipstick was called Cherries in the Snow, and underneath her white shirt she wore a black-lace bustier, which she claimed increased her tips. At the staff Christmas party she swished into the dining room in one of her mother's coming-out dresses from the fifties, cream tulle piped in black velvet, and I stared as the hem unraveled around her ankles.

McKenzie said I was precocious. She said I was an "old-fashioned dear." When it turned out we had the same birthday, February 26, she said we *had* to be friends. Sometimes she took me to her apartment. She had an old-fashioned white phone that never worked but looked cool, a red-velvet boudoir pillow, and a jewelry box. Inside the jewelry box she kept gilt-tipped powder puffs, stray feathers from an angel-white boa, black-lace garters, and blood-dark roses drooping off of split blue ribbons with ink-splotched messages from admirers. They must have been admirers, because McKenzie, I knew, went out on dates.

Once she asked me if I had ever had a boyfriend. "I'm only ten," I said.

"I had boyfriends," she told me, "long before that."

McKenzie made only one food: tomato and Boursin sandwiches on pumpernickel bread. Her mother never cooked anything else, either, she told me. McKenzie came from the South, from one of the Carolinas (I couldn't remember which one); her voice mingled gardenias and cigarettes. At the age of seventeen she'd run away and worked at a hot-dog stand behind the beach. I pictured her in a yellow gingham bikini, legs sprawled over the arm of a plastic fold-out chair, idly squeezing mustard onto the hot dogs. "I've been in the hospitality industry ever since," she said. "Or is it the *hostility* industry, darling?" She wanted to be an actress; it seemed like a lot of people in the front room did.

Setup began at three thirty. An hour before, McKenzie started to prepare for work. She had to put on the bustier at home, she explained, to get in the mood; I wondered what *the mood* meant. Whatever it was, it involved powder and mascara, and several coats of Cherries in the Snow. "Take note, my dear: it's the only red for blondes."

But I wasn't blond anymore, or not as blond as I had been. Strangers no longer cooed over my downy golden curls, because now they were only light brown, only ash. I couldn't wait till I was old enough to get highlights—like McKenzie's, like my mother's.

Meanwhile, McKenzie rubbed the powder onto her face while I sat on one of the red-velvet pillows on the floor. Then I remembered that my mother was going to a party tonight. I pictured the too-small bathroom of our latest apartment steaming from my mother's perfumed bubble bath. It was Saturday. We had two hundred and fifty reservations on the books. If I went to the restaurant, I would only be able to order an appetizer, and then I'd have to eat it in the office, making sure not to spill my food on the piles of bills.

I heard the yank of a zipper and the teeth scraping against the silk lining of McKenzie's bustier. "Come on," she said, buttoning up her cardigan. "I don't want to be late." So I dropped the garter in my hand and I followed her, back to the restaurant.

Several months later, my mother came home from work and said, "Charlotte, come out in the hall for a second. I have a present for you."

She had a knack for sudden gifts, my mother. Often she brought me home lilac sachets or Tiffany key chains, but I wondered what could be out in the hallway.

"It's big," she said. "I had to hire one of the guys in the kitchen to get it up the stairs."

We stepped out into the hallway. She told me to close my eyes, and when I opened them, I saw a vanity table. Pink-and-green silk ribbons dangled in front of the mirror. I had always longed for a vanity table.

"Thank you, Mummy, it's . . ."

"Isn't it a beauty? McKenzie thought you would like it." I tugged one of the ribbons. "It used to be McKenzie's," she said. "She wanted to get rid of it before the move."

I paused. Then I asked, "Where is she moving to this time?"

"Oh, LA. You know, for acting."

The ribbon slid to the floor. It didn't matter; there were other ribbons.

It was a Saturday morning, one of those long Saturday mornings when the dining room was empty and I had nothing to do. I stood on top of the chair outside the waiters' station, staring at the poster of the man with the top hat and fangs, and when I touched the case, dust caked my fingertips. Had Richard told the truth? Did the Pudding ghost live inside the frame? I couldn't find out yet, because ghosts didn't come out in the sunshine. We hadn't set the table for staff lunch yet and I hadn't seen anybody pop open a bottle of red wine. That's how early it was.

Moments passed, more dust blew off the poster case, and then I heard a scream from the kitchen, a scream that could have punctured the vaulted ceiling. Then I heard another one.

"A mouse!" my mother cried. "A mouse!"

"No, it's—" I heard Carla's voice.

"Oh, no, don't tell me it's a rat!"

"Fire!"

Mixing spoons and copper pots clattered against the floor. The dishwasher turned off his faucet. I was still standing on top of the chair and my knees wobbled.

"Charlotte," said Carla, thrusting open the double doors, "get out of here. Get out of here *now*."

"But my mother—"

"Your mother's *fine*. Now go!"

I jumped down from the chair. As I dashed through the dining room, I smelled smoke curling in the air. The black-painted doors had never felt so heavy to me as they did at that moment. I was alone as I fled down the staircase, and I could not hear anything, not even curses or screams, from upstairs. My mother—my mother might *die*. They all might die in the flames.

Outside, I crossed the street and stared at the building. I didn't see any flames, only smoke, plumes and plumes of smoke spiraling around the building. My mother was fine, Carla had said. She was fine. Holyoke Street was empty except for me, and I cried, I cried in great, racking sobs. Even later, when the fire trucks roared down the street and spectators had started to gather on the sidewalk, I was still crying.

The building had not burned down after all. The clouds of smoke thinned, and then the chefs slunk out from the alley. They leaned against the redbrick wall of 8 Holyoke Street in their bandannas and black-and-white-check pants, smoking while the firefighters sprayed their hoses. I crossed the street.

"You know," said Carla, pointing at the crowd, "leave it to those half-wits to blame it on the cigarettes. The firefighters told us something caught on fire in the pipes. Why not, kiddo? This building's fucking old."

Only the kitchen had been damaged; the dining room was safe. We reopened for business in a couple of weeks. But I have always remembered that fire, because it seemed to me the end of one era in the kitchen and the beginning of another when, not long afterward, Carla gave her resignation to my mother. She was the last person there who remained from my father's days, and the two of them had always been great friends. When she left, it felt like the last link to him had gone.

She gave her resignation right after Benny, her brown Doberman with the bullet in his leg, had to be put to sleep. After he died, my mother and I took Carla, who was already trashed on red wine, out to a twenty-four-hour pizza joint on Mass Ave once we had locked up the Pudding. She downed several beers and passed out over her bowl of spaghetti, and she did not show up for work ever again. My father, who occasionally picked up catering shifts, sometimes ran into her behind the scenes at these events, where she muttered to him in passing, "What is it about weddings and wild rice? Wild rice, wild rice—it's enough to make you never want to get married." Last we had heard, she was living with three lame dogs and her parents in Erie, Pennsylvania.

But in the restaurant business, nothing was forever. People on the staff were forever going away. They just up and left, sometimes with explanations but more often without. Sometimes we heard from them afterward and sometimes we did not. We learned that Patrick, the bartender who used to style my hair, didn't even have the same name anymore. He worked as the limousine driver at a monastery in Vermont, and now he called himself Tino Barbarossa. His parents had held a name-changing ceremony at their house, where his mother had spelled out the new name in deviled eggs on a platter. "What a lot of deviled eggs to make," my mother said. "Maybe I should hire *her* to be a line cook."

Charlie, the line cook with the three-piece violet suit that my mother had recruited from the homeless shelter, also left. After three years at the Pudding, he placed a personal ad, went on one date with a self-professed "songstress" named Rochelle (whose own ad, my mother later told me, was headed "Church-going woman loves oral sex"), and married her a month later in a gospel ceremony to which my mother was not invited; Rochelle had named her "the blond bitch." Charlie now dabbled in the real-estate business. Or he said he did; when he called my mother, drooling about some "sweet, sweet deal" he'd found for her, she could hear the murmur of the daytime soaps in the background.

"It's too bad," said my mother. "He had the real hospitality touch, Charlie did."

"Hospitality? But he worked *in the kitchen,*" I said. Kitchen people were not noted for their customer-friendly touch, and it was a blessing, in most cases, that they seldom interacted with the public.

"Oh, but I used to have him answer the phone in the mornings," my mother said. "You know, when the phone rang before anyone from the front room got in. Oh, he had the most wonderful phone manner of anybody; I wish I'd had him answering the phone all the time. Well, anyway, one morning I happened to overhear him. The person must have been asking him what kind of food did we serve because Charlie, without missing a beat, said"—and here my mother imitated his Southern accent—"'Well, ma'am, I do believe it's Polynesian.' *Polynesian? Polynesian?* But he sounded so lovely when he said it, I hardly had the heart to correct him."

Eight

FOOD OPPORTUNITIES

My mother liked to warn me about the food outside high-end restaurants. A machine tenderized the meat; the greens drooped; no one hand-rolled the pasta. They baked cakes from mixes and made mashed potatoes out of powder. "Never order chicken just anywhere," my mother told me. "They're filthy animals." The chickens we served at the Pudding, baked in their crackling golden skins and rubbed in fried sage, came from private farms. We knew all our suppliers by name, fed them biscotti while they waited for the check, and gave them gift certificates at Christmas. My mother air-kissed the woman who dug our Wellfleet clams out of the sea with her own hands and the man who foraged for our wild mushrooms in the woods. I could stare down at my plate and trace every ingredient—how could I go to another restaurant?

But food, what my mother called "beautiful, beautiful food," took time. It also took money. While we splurged on

ingredients at the restaurant, we saved at home; our refrigerator was empty, except for blue cans of seltzer water. My
mother left her lipstick around the edges of the turquoise
cans and littered them around our apartment, on top of
stacks of old newspapers or cookbooks or mixed in with the
plastic Chanel bangles on her vanity table. If we had a half
box of stale Cheerios, then we had no milk, or the milk
would be sour, or if the milk was fine then we had no Cheerios. Sometimes my mother brought home dishes from the
restaurant, but sometimes they did not travel well and I
had to pry Moulard duck breasts off of plastic containers
gelled over with burgundy-cherry sauce. Most nights that I
stayed home I depended on baked potatoes, salt, no butter.
I ate them alone on winter nights in my flannel nightgowns,
reading nineteenth-century Russian novels. My mother ate
baked potatoes, too, without the salt.

Because she made no apologies for the absence of food
in our home, my mother coined the phrase *food opportunities*. Food opportunities did not need to be beautiful; I simply had to seize them when they presented themselves. So I
ate, aside from my meals at the Pudding, a variety of food:
Chinese takeout and cheeseburgers with the staff, deviled
eggs and margaritas at people's summerhouses, drippy flans
and lukewarm cocoas from coffee shops in the Square. I also

ate the food at my classmates' houses. It tended, in Cambridge, to be drab and healthy: great tubs of ginger cous-
cous, tabouli with slivers of purple onions and sun-dried
tomatoes, bottles of Orangina and Perrier.

My mother didn't do school lunches. Instead, every
Sunday she brought home a dozen bagels and wrapped
them in tinfoil so they would keep for the rest of the week.
In the mornings she called me from the restaurant at seven
thirty—she went into the Square hours before—to wake
me up for school, and I stumbled into the kitchenette and
plopped one of the bagels into a brown paper bag. The bagel
was usually cinnamon-raisin, and stale. I didn't have any
chips or celery sticks to go with it, and at school I ate my
lunch fast, with an air of duty, as if I were popping a pill. I
only minded the lack of beverage. My mouth felt dry from
the whole wheat and sugary from the raisins, and I would as
soon use the water fountain, with hairs stuck to the metal
and pieces of bubble gum floating in the drain, as I would
eat a school lunch—the ones you bought, with the square-
shaped pizzas and spongy peas in the aluminum trays.

When I was in the fifth grade, I decided to ask my mother
if she could buy me some juice boxes, a package of juice
boxes that would last the whole week. The other girls had
juice boxes, and they got to prick straws through the holes

of the multicolored boxes and sip and sip. If I had a juice box, I could alternate my sips with bites from the bagel, and lunch would last much longer.

The day I finally asked her about the juice boxes, my mother had just come home from work. She had a cocktail party to go to in forty minutes, and she was moisturizing her legs. A pair of fishnets dangled off the arm of her stair-climber.

"Mummy," I said, standing at the foot of her bed, "if you go to the supermarket sometime, would you ever please buy me some juice boxes?"

Her expression looked the same as it had when I'd given her, at age six, the lopsided paper angel with a pipe-cleaner halo I'd made at the holiday arts and crafts fair. She was never much of a fan of childhood arts and crafts, my mother. *"Juice boxes"* was all she said, shaking her head. *"Juice boxes."*

The next day at school, I drank from the water fountain.

Sometimes on Sunday nights, my mother stayed home. That was the only time of the week she ever did. Then we both took hot baths and put on our flannel nightgowns, and she would make Benjamin and me a simple dish she used to make us at the farmhouse: poached eggs on English muffins. We ate them together at a wobbly-topped glass table, and those nights "keeping up with the conversation" didn't matter; there were no air kisses and no laughs. I read *Vogue*; she read the real-estate section of *The Boston Globe*. When she read, my mother took off her sunglasses, and I could see her eyes. They looked misty as she flicked the pages, and I knew she was thinking that all the prices were too high. She still couldn't afford to buy a house.

After she had prepped for brunch some Sundays, my mother would go to open houses. She looked at all sorts of houses, ones she could afford and ones she could not: brownstones in downtown Boston and two-families in Somerville and farmhouses like the one we had left years ago. She said she wanted her own garden and her own kitchen where, during snowstorms, she could bake brioche doughnuts as she had when I was a little girl. She said she wanted her own Christmas tree—a place to hang the hundreds of ornaments we kept in storage.

On some summertime Sunday afternoons, we would drive out to Bedford, where our farmhouse had been, so my mother could go to the farm stands there and in Concord. "I'm looking for potatoes," she said. "Beautiful Red Bliss potatoes I'll dip in some salt for dinner."

And then, from the bottom of her being, my mother would sigh, revealing a softness, a quality of yearning dissatisfaction, that she seldom exposed at the restaurant.

But what about money? Why did the restaurant never make any money? But it didn't. No matter how much business they did, there were too many expenses. The Pudding was simply on too lavish a scale. If you wanted to make money in the restaurant business, my mother said, the thing to do was open a pizza joint or maybe a Chinese take-out place. "Why didn't you?" I once asked her.

"Because I'm interested in the product," she said. "I'm interested in things being *beautiful.*"

So our lives, while unstable, were always also beautiful; the veneer of things, the shimmer of them, mattered. And so our lifestyle was always on a scale that our finances, strictly speaking, couldn't support.

One of the things that helped us to live this way was trade.

We had trade at stores in Harvard Square; that meant we gave people charge accounts at the Pudding in exchange for their services. We had trade at Harvard Book Store and Colonial Drug and Casablanca, the bar next to the Brattle Theatre. We had trade with Serge the florist and trade at Gino, the hair salon down the street where the bill for my mother's highlights, which she brightened every three months, cost hundreds of dollars. Our tailor dined at the

Pudding on trade. So did my mother's lawyers, her exterminator, manicurist, and house inspector. I later on had a ther-
apist who dined on trade.

Meanwhile, at the Pudding, we simply replaced instead
of washed the linens, we tossed the leftover veal chops in
the garbage at the end of the night, and my mother dished
out thousands of dollars during the holidays on all the employee bonuses alone. "Oh, well," she said, shrugging. "Fine
dining should be like a great dinner party at someone's
house and, if you want *my* opinion, nobody has fun if the
hostess worries about spilling red wine on the carpet." To
dine at the Pudding *was* like going to a dinner party: people
often ate for free. Indeed, freebies swirled in the dining
room like confetti.

"Trade," my mother said. "It makes the world go round."

And so, for us, for many years, it did.

On Friday nights I used to go visit my father's studio. I
remember one evening during the height of summertime when he pulled up on the curb in his latest crummy,
wheezing old car and got out to greet me. He wore a pair of
denim shorts coarsely cut off below the knee. I thought to
myself, *Oh, no. Not the denim shorts.* The paint-splattered
black pants were bad enough.

But then, I was dressed pretty shabbily myself. I always made a point of wearing my oldest clothes whenever I saw my father, because that way I didn't mind if they ended up smelling like cigarettes.

My father and I decided to go to dinner at a vegetarian restaurant in Harvard Square, a restaurant that isn't there anymore. We waited in line to be seated. The hostess did a double take when she saw us. Then, in a tone of exaggerated friendliness, she said, "Oh, come right this way with me. You must be so hungry," she added gently to me. And all at once it clicked: She had seen my father. She had seen the denim shorts. The cigarettes, the seedy air of poverty. She thought that we were homeless people.

My mother, meanwhile, had quite a tolerant attitude toward the homeless people in Harvard Square. Indeed, she felt something of an affinity with them. "No one's even up in Harvard Square when I get to the restaurant. It's just me and the homeless people."

It showed a certain entrepreneurial spirit to have claimed territory in the Square as your own without even paying for it, my mother always said, and she respected the homeless. She thought the man who sold *Spare Change* in front of Au Bon Pain, waving the newspapers in pedestrians' faces and calling, in a resounding Southern accent, *"Young lady, young lady,"* was a wonderful salesman. Every time she walked past him she nodded, as if to congratulate him. "He's got hustle," she told me. "That's what I look for." Another homeless person stole my mother's *New York Times* off the front steps every morning, and when she found out his identity, instead of scolding him, she asked him why, with such a consistent record of early rising, he couldn't get a job. "He must be a kitchen person," she said. "Most waiters can barely drag themselves to a ten o'clock brunch shift."

The Pudding bathroom, located on the second floor of an open building, was one of the only accessible bathrooms in the Square, and homeless people used it all the time. Sometimes they flooded the bathroom with water, trying to clean themselves, and when a member of the staff alerted my mother to the gushing faucets, she turned them off and gave the person a cup of coffee and whatever cookies we had available in the kitchen. If they vomited on the floor, as they often did, my mother mopped up the puddles. "I don't mind," she said, "as long as it's *their* vomit and not the vomit of the Hasty Pudding kids."

One morning, when she was alone in the kitchen, a man in a ski mask crept up the back stairs. Afterward, she calmly reported the incident to the staff. "I told him," she later said, "never to mess with women in kitchens again."

In the end, it was not the man in the ski mask but an obese woman known among the staff as Fatty-Pie who gave

my mother the most trouble out of all the homeless people. Fatty-Pie sat on a milk crate outside of Yenching Restaurant on the corner of Holyoke Street and Mass Ave; her
sign read PLEASE HELP—SOBER—CHRISTIAN—HUNGRY.
My mother considered herself an authority on Fatty-Pie,
who had stolen her milk crate from behind the Pudding
Dumpster, and early one morning, when she was walking
down Holyoke Street, she discovered that there were *two*
Fatty-Pies: one got into a car and the other stepped out.
They also used the Pudding bathroom, and once my mother
found one of the twins eating Twinkies in the handicapped
stall. "Heavens," she said later that night, pressing her hand
over her heart. "I'll let you imagine the rest of the details for
yourself."

Then one Saturday night during the eight o'clock rush,
Fatty-Pie, in a pair of jade green sweatpants and a baseball
cap, barged into the dining room, waving a piece of paper in
the air. It turned out to be an eight-hundred-dollar gift certificate to the Pudding, issued in the name of a waiter whom
my mother had recently fired for missing his shifts. The
waiter, in a dazzling act of revenge, had presented the gift
certificate to Fatty-Pie, knowing that my mother had tried
to ban her from the building and that she would try to use
it. But even he couldn't have predicted her persistence;

when the hostess refused to seat her, she asked if she could redeem the gift certificate in cash.

"I wonder," my mother exclaimed after the woman had left the building, "*which* Fatty-Pie that was!"

*E*ven though our financial situation was often uncertain, my mother continued to buy me, sparing no expense, the most beautiful party dresses. The turning of the seasons was signified by going to the children's department at Neiman Marcus, where all of the salesladies knew my name.

Holidays were signified by different dresses: rust-colored taffeta for Thanksgiving, black velvet for Christmas. One Easter dress in particular I remember: navy grosgrain with white polka dots and a chiffon sailor collar, one of the prettiest dresses I ever had.

"Oh, Mummy," I said, doing a little twirl in front of the mirror, "can I wear it to Easter brunch?"

"It's *perfect* for Easter. With your navy Mary Janes."

But though my mother and I made much of what I was going to wear on any given holiday, when the holiday actually came, it was another story. My mother would be so busy at the restaurant, she would be much too preoccupied to pay attention to what I was wearing or what I was going to do that day.

That Easter, it rained. But I wanted to wear my new party dress anyway. I fluffed the chiffon collar over my shoulders, buckled my Mary Janes, and snapped up the buttons of my pink rain slicker. Then I walked into Harvard Square by myself. The rain slicker didn't have a hood, and rain pattered down on my braids and soaked through the white ribbons at the tips. By the time I got out of Harvard Yard, all I wanted was fresh orange juice squeezed the way I liked, in a martini glass, and a plate of smoked salmon on buttered toast. Everything would be fine, once I sat down at the table with my mother.

There was no hostess at the top of the stairs, and when I opened the door to the dining room and saw the rows and rows of full tables, I remembered that everyone in the restaurant business hated Easter, as they hated most holidays. Everyone already hated brunch, and this was brunch with old people and children. Looking around the dining room, I saw only families: blue-haired grandmothers peering at the menu through thick glasses, grandfathers in navy blazers with gold buttons, mothers and fathers sitting next to each other and sharing menus, little boys in wool shorts that buttoned on the side. I also saw other little girls whose dresses, I was certain, were not as stylish as mine.

These children, I noticed, had a hard time sitting still at the table with the grown-ups. They spit out maraschino cherries onto their bread plates and tapped their feet against the carpet while the adults read the menu to them and buttered their scones. Then a group of children scuttled past me, giggling and sprinkling jelly beans onto the carpet. I moved out of their way, like I moved out of the waiters' way during the eight o'clock crunch on Saturday nights, and the children glanced at me as if I were just another object in the dining room: a champagne bucket or a vase.

At the four-top next to me, the mother was talking to the waiter and pointing to the plate of pasta in front of her child. The pasta was all white, except for some cheese grated on top. We did not offer plain pasta on the menu.

"It's just Parmesan," I heard the waiter say. "I think the chefs just add it out of habit—"

"I'm sorry. It's just, she'll only eat plain noodles."

"I'll get you another plate, then."

Then another waiter darted past me, receipts in hand. "Separate checks," I heard him say. "They *would* ask for separate checks." He paused when he saw me. "Hey," he said, "do you know if your mother is coming back in today?"

"She's not home," I said. "She's in the kitchen."

"No, she left just a little—" He squinted at the numbers printed out on one of the receipts. "Honestly, she was here all night. Hand-molding all these stupid dark-chocolate bunnies."

I had wanted one of the dark-chocolate bunnies for dessert. Then I pictured my mother's apron, sooty with Valrhona, tangled at the foot of her bed. She would be running the tub now. She would want to be alone. I could hear her voice: "Charlotte, I am *not* the Entertainment Committee."

I followed the waiter into the office, where he swiped credit cards through the machine. "Pretty dress," he said finally. "Are you going somewhere or something? The dining room's full today."

He whizzed out of the office. I sank into a chair and picked up the phone; maybe my father was home. I dialed the number and hoped he would answer. Sometimes he didn't answer—sometimes he paced the creaking floors of his studio for days and days, mixing chemicals and snapping close-ups of a favorite object until he ran out of film.

"Hello," he said. His voice, as always, wheezed, and was followed by a cough. Recently, people had begun saying to me, "Charlotte! Your father's voice." What they meant was that he should stop smoking, though I knew he never would.

"It's me," I said. "I thought maybe we could get together today, if you aren't busy."

"Oh, sure, Char," he said. "You at the restaurant?"

"Yeah, it's Easter brunch, and there are all these families in the dining room. No place to sit down."

"Oh, Christ, holidays in the restaurant business! I'm so glad I don't have to work them anymore. Though is there lamb on the menu, for Easter? I do make a hell of a rack of lamb. Well, anyway. I'll go and get you, Char."

My father showed up, and he took me and my party dress to lunch at The Tasty. Always one of his favorites, it was where he used to go late at night, after he locked up the Pudding.

We sat down at the counter. My father ordered a fried-egg sandwich and a Coke; I ordered pumpernickel toast and a glass of ice water. The toast was prebuttered and came with tiny packages of grape jelly. It struck me as exotic and delightful, the way that package after package of those tiny grape jellies were all identical. So different from the food at the Pudding, which was so subject to the individual hand of the chef behind the line that night; and my father's hand, everybody still said, had been the lightest and most deft of all. "Your father . . . ," my mother would say, recalling a dish of his. And then she would sigh.

Maybe he noticed me staring at the package of grape jelly, because he said, "You know, Fiona"—naming a friend of his whom I thought very glamorous, a white-skinned, flame-haired, lapsed Irish Catholic, a fellow artist and chain-smoker with a penchant for fishnet stockings and flasks of whiskey—"loves airplane food, did she ever tell you that? She says it's so exciting, the way you have to unwrap all those little mystery packages. She says it's like opening jewelry!"

"That sounds just like Fiona," I said. The last time I had seen her, at an open studio of my father's, she had regaled me with the tale of having to leave the Catholic Church as soon as she hit puberty, for sex, she could tell, was going to be her great temptation. I was fascinated by her silver lipstick, rather corpselike, I thought, and in keeping with the haunted feeling of my father's photographs.

"Doesn't it, though?" said my father, and he laughed. Fiona was exactly the kind of "character" he liked to keep around. "Hey, think I'll get another sandwich. And more coffee. Rainy days are so great for sitting around and drinking bad diner coffee. There's a certain kind of day where *bad* coffee actually hits the spot more than *good* coffee, you know?"

When the sandwich arrived, he bit into it and said, "These are some damn good sandwiches. Better than anything we ever served at the Pudding, if you ask me."

And so we sat there, safe inside The Tasty, as outside the rain crashed down.

With my father, there was never any shortage of food opportunities, and sometimes on Friday nights we went to Savenor's together. He would pick me up at our apartment building and we would go across the street to get cold cuts. Jack Savenor, the owner, had taught both my parents how to butcher in their Peasant Stock days, and he never complained when the Pudding had overdue bills. When we went into the store, he gave us samples from the back: artichoke petals scattered in olive oil, clumps of Boursin in brown paper napkins, and, when it was available, freshly cut slices of smoked pheasant, because my father had told him that was my favorite. My favorite appetizer of my father's, back when he was still the chef at the Pudding, was smoked pheasant and Roquefort flan.

"Thank you, Mr. Savenor," I said, standing at the foot of the glass counter. The blackboard loomed above me. It said, in orange chalk: OSTRICH. TURTLE. BOAR.

"This daughter of yours is too damn polite," he said to my father, wiping a film of spit off his chin. "Tell her to call me Jack already."

Jack, I feared, was too friendly. I didn't want to give him the wrong idea. When we ran into him on the street, he squeezed my mother's waist and kissed her smack on the mouth. She laughed and kissed him back, but what if he kissed *me*? He was very old and very red—was it the flush on his face or the blood? Blood was everywhere: it seeped through his white coat and smeared his thick fingertips. He liked to tell my father filthy stories, like the one about the time when he was butchering skirt steak and the knife had slipped and, he claimed, pierced his testicles.

"Cock and balls," he said. "Now you just picture *that.* Made prime rib juices look like lemon vinaigrette, you following me?"

Mrs. Savenor, his mother, was even older. She was also immense. Before she had immigrated to America and opened the store, she used to smuggle cigarettes over the Russian border, and she had kept her business know-how to this day. She glowered behind the cash register, scooping smoked herring out of a jar and talking to customers as the fishy juices trickled down her chin so they would panic and leave their change on the counter. It was rumored that she bought a new car every year with the change customers had left behind. Even Jack feared her. My father said that he carried a thousand dollars cash in the pocket of his butcher's coat at all times, because he was convinced she would swindle him out of his wages.

Only customers got swindled. Jack was called "the man with the golden thumb," because he always put his finger on the scale to up the price. Suburban housewives, who had read that Julia Child used Jack as her butcher, flocked to Savenor's to buy meat for their dinner parties. Afterward, when Jack had given them a tour of the back and kissed their hands, "they would pay for bologna as if it were ostrich," my father said. But we did not get swindled, and sometimes Mrs. Savenor slipped lollipops in strange flavors—cherry cola or piña colada or maple—into our grocery bags.

When we got to my father's studio, we ate dinner at a small wooden table, one of the only pieces of furniture in the whole room. "That Jack Savenor," my father said, ripping open the tissue paper around our slices of rare roast beef, "is the best goddamn butcher in the world."

Afterward, we ate root beer floats and watched old movies. We watched *L'Avventura* or *Cries and Whispers* or *Bicycle Thieves*. And when the movie was over and my father went back to his artwork again, squinting with a rapt, hungry expression at a negative drying on a string, I entertained myself by exploring his collection of antique cameras. His most prized possession was a twenty-by-twenty-four-feet Robertson process camera, so big it could fill a small-sized room. I used to hide underneath its black velvet crinkles and folds, letting the weight of the material enfold me.

My father during this period was feverishly artistically productive. In 1990 he had a show at the Fogg Art Museum at Harvard. In his artist's statement he wrote, "I wanted to see what it was like to live inside a painting . . . I painted every day." In a sense, he succeeded in doing just that: transforming the walls of his studio into a perpetually changing canvas. He loved painting them different colors. Every month, portions of the walls of his studio turned from silver to Chinese red, pitch-black to Prussian blue. That silver, though, was his favorite color. He returned to it again and again. But when I called it "silver," he insisted on calling it "invisible."

"There's no such thing as invisible," I said. And then, anxious to differentiate myself from him, "*My* favorite color is pink."

"Well, everybody already knows *that*, Char," my father said, laughing. "I'm not that big on pink, myself."

"There's no such thing as invisible. Invisible means you can't see it."

"Oh, yes there is," said my father. "It's one hell of a color, Char. You ought to see it one of these days."

My father was friends with the avant-garde composer

John Cage, whose theories didn't make much sense to me, either. Sometimes John came to lunch at the studio, where my father was doing a series of portraits of him. All I remember of him was that he was very old and, though my father said he was very famous, not at all fancy. He wore a denim work outfit and spoke few words. We sat at the table eating herrings in cream. The conversation at the table bored me, and I used to get up in the middle of the meal and spin around the studio, a thing I liked to do in those days. That studio was a marvelous open space for spinning. While I spun, I always talked to myself under my breath, making up stories, but neither my father nor John Cage minded: that was the nice thing about them.

When I was eleven years old, Savenor's burned to the ground.

The night of the fire, I awoke smelling smoke from outside my window. It thickened and swirled on our balcony, and when I slid open the door and stepped outside, I saw flames across the street. Trucks thundered down the street, sirens screeched, and customers from the bar next door thronged the sidewalks. I was beginning to cough, and then I spotted a drift of white chiffon that blended with the smoke. My mother had put on a white chiffon cape earlier that evening, when she had left for a cocktail party, and now she was on her way home. She watched, along with the rest of the crowd, as the store where, once upon a time, she and my father had learned to butcher collapsed in flames.

Later that night, I heard my mother's sobs as she peeled off her cocktail dress, but the next morning when I got up to go to school she had already left for work. I packed my cinnamon-raisin bagel in a paper bag and walked outside. So it had not been a nightmare. Across the street where Savenor's had still stood only the night before was a mountain of ashes.

After the fire, the neighborhood changed. New businesses sprang up: a trendy bakery, an upscale catering company, a noodle joint. Now when he picked me up on Friday nights, my father would survey the site where Savenor's had once been and mutter, taking a mournful drag of his cigarette, "I tell you what, Char: I *do* miss that roast beef."

I missed Savenor's, too. I missed the food opportunities, the pieces of pheasant and Boursin in brown paper towels and piña colada lollipops. I missed the comforting routine of the produce trucks pulling up, same as they did every day on Holyoke Street, across from our apartment building. I even missed Jack Savenor himself, strutting down the street in his blood-soaked coat, though the Savenors, from all accounts, recovered after the fire and opened another store on Beacon Hill.

It seems to me now that the end of Savenor's was also the end of those Friday nights with my father. We still saw each other sometimes; we went other places, ate other food. But there was never the same sense of ritual—the sacredness of sharing food opportunities, father and daughter, together— now that Savenor's was no more.

Nine

THE DEAD PARENTS CLUB

$\mathcal{S}$ensitive? Sensitive? I haven't been sensitive since 1967."

One afternoon, I was sitting at A-1 when my mother slammed the receiver down on the tabletop. The dial tone sounded in the dining room, and she hung up the phone properly. Then she hacked the greens of her Caesar salad in half and shoveled her croutons onto my bread plate as usual.

"So this pastry chef—this ex-pastry chef—that was her on the phone. 'You don't run a very sensitive kitchen,' she told me. And I said—"

"I heard you, Mummy. I heard."

"She's one of those culinary-school types," she said. "Wants to wear a monogrammed coat and flounce around and never get dirty. She calls this her *career*. It's a job. You get up and you go and . . ." She glanced at my plate. "What's the matter? Something wrong with your salmon?"

Something *was* wrong with the salmon: it was mediocre. It was a bumpy time at the Pudding. *The Boston Globe* had given us a three-and-a-half-star review—our first one under four since the restaurant had opened—and the critic compared the dining experience to "stepping into the third installment of *Brideshead Revisited*." "That is *not* a compliment, Charlotte," my mother told me, even though I myself was a big fan of the book. She attributed the problem to the staff in the kitchen, not the front room. "The front room is always a drag," she said. "The kitchen is what changes."

Just recently, my mother and Mary-Catherine had journeyed to Vermont, where a friend of theirs had recommended that they hire a chef from a restaurant called Smoke Jack's who was said to be interested in leaving Vermont and moving to Boston. My mother, desperate to find someone, hired the chef against her better judgment. Things didn't work out, resulting in what my mother referred to as "one of those little conversations," which was her euphemism for firing people. (Her euphemism for substance abuse was "that little problem with which we're so familiar.") Afterward, she remarked to Mary-Catherine, "What the hell was the matter with us, going all the way up to Vermont like idiots, looking for talent at someplace called Smoke Jack's?" My mother shuddered at the memory. "Smoke Jack's! If that doesn't show absolute failure of judgment, then I don't know what does."

During this time, my mother started hiring more and more people from the homeless shelter, the Pine Street Inn, in downtown Boston. They worked fourteen-hour days five days a week, and then sometimes, after they received their paychecks on Friday afternoon, they didn't show for Saturday prep. On Monday morning they appeared at seven o'clock sharp and explained to my mother that there had been a sudden death in the family. "It was always a great-aunt," she said. "And her name was always Aunt Eulalie or Aunt Delilah, and they were always taking buses to South Carolina or Georgia, and expecting me to believe they'd made it there and back by Monday morning." In response, she founded the Dead Parents Club. This was more of a policy than a club, and it meant that for a period she only hired people whose immediate relatives had died.

Despite the Dead Parents Club, and my mother's warning "Call in sick or call in dead," employees still missed their shifts. You could lose a waiter or even a chef, she said, but never a dishwasher. If such an emergency occurred, she stalked over to the Pit, the Harvard Square gathering place for punks and delinquents between Out of Town News and the subway station, and called out, "Want to make money?

Come wash dishes with me." Anyone who happened to be hanging out there was welcome, she said, except the boy who kept the white rat on a chain.

Finally, it was the Colombian immigrants and not the delinquents who saved the kitchen. The Colombians worked hard, and their complaints, if they had any, were not in English. My mother learned only one Spanish word—¡pronto! meaning *hurry!*—and claimed she needed no others to communicate to the prep cooks, who julienned vegetables as well as the culinary-school graduates. The Colombians brought over their brothers and cousins and got them jobs at the Pudding, too. Soon the "family meals" at the Pudding featured not pastrami sandwiches from Elsie's but shrimp tacos and rice and beans.

My mother loved the Colombians, and she spent more time with them, she herself admitted, than she ever had with me. The prep cooks arrived at six o'clock in the morning, and after two hours alone, kneading dough in the drafty kitchen, she must have craved their company. They ate breakfast together on the milk crates on the fire escape; they scrambled the eggs and she sliced the pancetta. Their work ethic resembled her own. "It's a wonder I'm not an immigrant," she told me, "the way I hustle."

As more and more South Americans joined the staff,

both in the kitchen and the front room, Harvard Real Estate wrote a letter to my mother asking the help to use the back door to the building. It didn't look proper, they said. Too many people hung about the entrance. Actually, it was mostly Hasty Pudding Club members in their telltale khakis and blue blazers who hung about there. The staff simply climbed the stairs and went to work. "Men in suits," my mother said, and although she kept most scraps of paper in a pile at the bottom of her pocketbook, she tossed this letter in the trash.

Whenever my mother saw a representative from Harvard Real Estate come into the dining room, her shoulders stiffened and, all of a sudden, she looked very small. I would remember that she was only five feet one; usually, because of her high heels and the extravagance of her personality, I forgot. These visits from Harvard Real Estate startled me every time. I looked at the "men in suits" and then at the dining room and knew that they could take it all away from us; they had that power. They just sat there with their clipboards, waiting for my mother to go over and talk business. I never knew about what exactly. Maybe they were there to raise the rent, or to negotiate a new lease. Or to express their displeasure with us as tenants, in some capacity or another.

Meanwhile, the Hasty Pudding kids had the run of the building. The annual Leather and Lace party was the highlight of their social season, second only to the excitement of the Man and Woman of the Year celebrations every February. That night if I happened to go into the building, it was not unusual to pass strapping members of the Harvard crew team strutting around in leather chaps and studded collars.

Mary-Catherine was always more fond of the Hasty Pudding kids than my mother ever was. The romantic sort, she had a soft spot for young men with nice manners who wore bow ties, whereas they exasperated my mother. A phrase my mother used with relish, when describing the tension in the building between the club and the restaurant, was *class warfare.*

"Oh, Deborah," Mary-Catherine would say, not buying it.

"Oh, Mary-Catherine," my mother said right back at her. "I can never get over how apolitical you are. Your idea of a political platform is *What is the candidate's position on the arts? What have they done lately for the good of classical music?"*

"Well, and why not? It's through the arts that a civilization—"

"Honest to God! Sometimes I think you didn't even *live* through the sixties."

*I*n the very beginning, the Pudding had been open only for dinner. Later, to get more business, we opened for lunch six days a week, and eventually, around when I was nine, for Sunday brunch, too. The Pudding being open for business earlier in the day meant that I no longer ever had the dining room to myself.

Even the Club Bar, where before I had danced on the diamonds and blown dust off the barstools for whole afternoons, was off-limits. At the suggestion of Harvard Real Estate, we locked it now, and only my mother, Mary-Catherine, and the managers had keys. We held weddings there, and bat mitzvahs and Christmas parties and business luncheons, and sometimes the managers gave people tours of the Club Bar, as if it were a condominium on the market, while they cooed over the red walls and the crocodiles. Every Thursday, the Hasty Pudding members ate lunch there, and sometimes the Krokodiloes practiced in front of the fireplace.

But beyond that, the dining room itself had changed. My mother, who long ago had replaced her cashmere kilts with black taffeta circle skirts, had similarly transformed the decor of the Pudding dining room by repainting the white wainscoting with red and gold stripes and placing leopard-print lamps at the bar. When the fire department banned candles in restaurants, she strung pink Christmas lights from the ceiling and attached pink crystal hearts to tissue stars. Glamorous—the restaurant looked glamorous now, but I missed the old dining room, where patches of oak had shown through the white wainscoting and where the pewter chandeliers had cast the brightest light.

"If only I could get rid of these heavy green walls," she said. "Imagine these walls pink, Charlotte. The perfect, soft, smudged pink." She also thought the posters could use gold frames instead of oak, but Harvard insisted the walls and the posters remain the same. The color pink, they told her, did not reflect the history of the Hasty Pudding Club. "That's what they think," she said. "Every other man who walks into this building is a pansy."

And the bar—it had changed, too. We had replaced the bottles of soda with a machine, which required the bartender to push red buttons labeled GINGER ALE or COKE so the liquid would spurt into the glasses. Instead of scooping ice out of the ancient ice machine in the Club Bar, which rumbled when it turned on and off, we dumped bags of ice into a red plastic cooler. I remembered the miniature bottles of maraschino cherries I had hoarded during my childhood, with the glossy red tops that had left my wrists sore after I twisted them off. But now we bought large bottles and stored the cherries, along with the lime wedges and orange twists, in shallow plastic trays where the bartender could reach them easily. The bar was more efficient now, everybody said.

My mother had also convinced our investors to finance the addition of an herb-garden terrace. Business had always lagged in the summer, but she thought customers would flock to any restaurant where they could dine outside. She was right: the addition of the terrace, located to the left of the dining room on the roof where we used to store milk crates and chill bottles of champagne, turned the summer months into the busiest of the year. She hand-painted the planks of the floor periwinkle blue, hung a violet silk canopy from the beams to block out the sunlight during lunch, grew only pink flowers, and wound pink Christmas lights through the leaves of the topiary trees. A green-stemmed stone fountain trickled in the corner, and white marble cherubs peeked out of flowerpots. *Romantic* was how people described the terrace.

Now, in the summertime, customers who never would have dined at the Pudding at all came to sit on the terrace. "We'd like a table for two," they told the hostess, *"on the terrace."* If they got seated in the dining room instead, they slumped into their ballroom chairs as if they had been banished from first class to coach. As for me, I never felt the same affection for the terrace that I felt for the dining room. The waitstaff crammed the tables close together, pigeons swooped over the plates, and the sounds of the kitchen—the clanks of pots and pans and the hiss of the dishwasher and curses and snatches of Spanish—swelled through the walls and spilled onto the deck. I dined on the terrace only on Saturday nights in the fall, when customers preferred the dining room to the cold, and by dessert I had to slip a tablecloth over my shoulders. And although the terrace had improved business, the Pudding was still losing money—the money just went. It went other places.

We also installed, due to disability-rights laws, an elevator. "We didn't have handicapped access before the elevator," my mother said, "and, believe me, we don't have it now, either." It was the cheapest model that could pass the safety inspection, and if someone wanted to use it, the hostess had to arrange for it to land on the right floor. It was also small, and the walls and ceiling were painted a scorching red. In the summer, the heat steamed up from beneath the carpet and left the passengers faint. The elevator occasionally broke down with people in it, and once my mother got stuck between the second and third floors with six crates of red snapper and two waiters. In spite of the smell of the fish, "It was the *waiters* I minded," she said. "The whole time they were whining for their cigarettes."

Even our logo was different. Instead of the dark green staircase with balloons floating over it, our menus and business cards showed a cartoon crocodile, modeled after the ones Teddy Roosevelt had shot, sitting at a table covered with pink linen. That crocodile also lounged on love seats, sipped Kir Royales, and blew out birthday candles. Pink stars, like the ones swinging from the dining room ceiling, sprinkled the background of every illustration. But I missed the dark green cursive on the old menus, missed filling in the balloons with the pink highlighters I had stolen from the desk drawers in the office. And I missed our old T-shirts, the green ones with the white staircases on the back. The white ones with pink letters looked, like the leopard lampshades, too new.

As business increased at the Pudding, the rules tightened. Health inspectors, who had shown up once a year causing panic, now paid regular visits, and my mother removed all steak tartare and carpaccio from the menu because she feared the possibility of citations of contamination. As for cigarettes behind the line, the city of Cambridge had passed a no-smoking law for restaurants. The chefs now smoked in the parking lot behind the alley, slumped on top of milk crates, gobbling Bolognese out of coffee cups.

I remembered the staff lunches of my childhood when everyone in the kitchen, from the dishwashers to my parents, had lounged in the front room, swilling Chianti and eating pastrami sandwiches from Elsie's. But Elsie's was now a chain called The Wrap that served sandwiches in sheaths of tinfoil stamped with typewritten labels and smoothies called Berry Blast and Banana Bliss. Now no one sent me out for sandwiches of any kind, and it seemed I had not seen anyone but customers drink red wine in years.

What had happened? Had *everyone* gone to rehab? My mother and Mary-Catherine no longer sent champagne to VIPs; they sent oysters, or pizza, because they never knew who could drink and who could not. Once, in a fit of delight, my mother comped the meal of a stranger who had ordered steak and Scotch for lunch, exclaiming, "Don't you understand? Steak and scotch! Nobody orders that anymore." Many members of the staff now preferred Diet Coke to beer, and my mother joked about posting a sign behind the line that read PLEASE DON'T SPEAK TO THE WAITERS UNTIL THEY HAVE TAKEN THEIR MEDICATIONS. For the employees who still drank, she made up a two-drink-per-shift law, so now they crept down the stairs to the Club Bar and swigged shots of vodka in the dark. Eventually, it seemed, they went to rehab, too, and took up yoga and progressive child care and whole-grain diets. "We often find," my mother said, "that after Upstairs at the Pudding, people tend to gravitate to those healing professions."

And ever since the Cambridge Fire Department had banned real trees in restaurants and we'd replaced the real tree with a fake one, Christmas just wasn't the same anymore. For one thing, the staff no longer made their own ornaments. And, without the magical fragrance of the real tree perfuming the dining room, summoning the holiday spirit took more work than usual. My mother bought strands of multicolored beads that looked like glazed Froot Loops on a string. And lights: she bought ropes of pink Christmas lights by the dozen, which she strung from the beams in the ceiling. The dining room no longer smelled of pine but of plastic.

Then, around the time I was in middle school, we no longer had the Christmas party, either. Now we had, the first week of January, an event simply called "the staff party." It took place in both the Club Bar and the dining room because the staff was so large, and instead of buying fast-food chicken wings and Twinkies, as my father had before, my mother hired a caterer. Most of all, I disliked the addition of the DJ, who played pulsing dance tunes in the Club Bar. The waiters asked me to dance, but every year I refused. Standing at the top of the staircase and peering at the members of the staff, some of whose names I had never learned at all, I remembered how in my childhood I, too, had danced on those very diamonds. But I was older now, and I stood still.

Yes, everything, everything had changed. Except for one thing: the lease. My mother still fretted about the lease and about money in general.

"But aren't we busy?"

"Oh, we're one of the busiest restaurants in the city. That's what the produce guys tell me."

I wanted to ask about money. Why didn't we make any money? But it would have been disrespectful to how hard my mother and Mary-Catherine worked to ask. And putting the question into words would only have confirmed what I already, deep in my bones, knew.

To me, nothing showed how much times had changed more than the disappearance of the charlotte au chocolat. (It still appeared at weddings and special events, but was no longer available on the regular menu.) This came about when my mother stopped baking the desserts herself and hired a procession of young pastry chefs. These pastry chefs had gone to culinary school, and apparently they didn't understand charlotte au chocolat. It was an old-fashioned dessert, whose beauty spoke for itself; it didn't need any frills. But the pastry chefs liked embellishing desserts with frills now: star-shaped cookies and chocolate cigarettes and spun sugar that looked like golden spiderwebs. Now, whenever I ordered dessert, I chose from clementine granita with red-wine-poached pears, almond cake trimmed with candied orange rind, or triple-crème cheesecakes, soft and dripping with huckleberry sauce. Charlotte au chocolat was gone.

Ten

CABARET
NIGHT

$\mathcal{A}$ Sunday night in April when I was twelve years old: it was still cold and not yet spring. Walking down Holyoke Street, I passed the restaurant, but didn't go in; I kept on walking because I had always liked this kind of weather, when a light mist fizzed in the air and the forsythia, just beginning to come out, formed ghostly yellow shapes against the gray. It was that time of year when my mother's fava-bean soup had just appeared on the menu; soon there would be fiddlehead ferns and strawberry ices. I stopped in front of the window of the Andover Shop, the men's clothing store at 22 Holyoke. I liked to look at the coral and lemon-drop cashmeres, the duck-handled umbrellas, the camel's-hair blazers, and the lushly fringed tartan scarves.

But tonight, tonight was different. Tonight I looked at these things and thought, *One day I will have a man in my life. One day I will buy things like this for him.*

It never occurred to me to buy such things for my father.

He shopped at a clothing warehouse called Dollar-a-Pound and gave the impression that he preferred it over all other options, expense aside. "You've got to see it, Char," he would say. "It's great. They throw all the clothes on the floor, and then you just go for it. None of that department-store bullshit."

The mist felt wonderful on my skin. Underneath my raincoat I was wearing a black velvet dress, my first grown-up dress; that is, the first dress of mine that came from the grown-ups' department and not the children's.

I turned and walked down Holyoke Street back toward the restaurant. Stepping into the building, I heard music rolling dreamily out of the doors of the Club Bar and down to the landing. It was Cabaret Night, another one of the new developments at the Pudding. My mother had gotten the idea to turn the Club Bar into a supper club with live music on Sunday nights in the wintertime. The Cabaret Night menu offered the swanky signature dishes of another era, things like oysters Rockefeller and shrimp cocktail with remoulade and chicken hash on toast points. The names of the drinks on the special cocktail menu were almost painterly: Golden Cadillacs, Pink Ladies, Blue Dreams, Lillet Blondes.

I can't give you anything but love, baby, the singer that

night was singing. She stood in front of the fireplace at the end of the room, underneath the famous crocodiles Teddy Roosevelt shot, wearing a long shimmery gown. *That's the only thing I've plenty of . . .*

At the bar I ordered a Brandy Alexander and a glass of vino. The singer crooned, *Gee, I'd like to see you looking swell, baby. Diamond bracelets Woolworth doesn't sell, baby . . .*

The Brandy Alexander was for me; the wine for Veronica, a dear family friend—my parents had known her as far back as the Peasant Stock days—who worked as a coatcheck girl at the Pudding on Cabaret Nights. Sunday was now my favorite night of the week because I got to visit with her.

I had a thing for Brandy Alexanders because my friends Henry and Alex used to let me have sips of theirs, nursing alcohol through rivers of heavy cream. Veronica preferred red wine, which she always called, in the Italian fashion, vino. I copied her.

Veronica, a former *Mademoiselle* cover girl and Avedon model, was keen on all things Italian: wines, men, and tailoring. She got all of her Italian clothing on deep, thrilling discount at the old Filene's Basement, where my mother used to get a lot of her designer clothing, too. I went with her sometimes; we prowled the racks. I can still see Veronica, eyes flashing, elbows akimbo, in the cramped and dingy aisles. She'd emerge out of the chaos triumphant with midnight blue suits with peplums, black velvet evening gowns out of a Sargent painting.

Veronica was a tall brunette with cut-glass bone structure who looked, as somebody once remarked to me, "like a cross between an angel and a witch." My father used to photograph her sometimes, her spiky, rather scary beauty a fitting subject for his platinum prints.

My father was a little bit in love with Veronica, in love with her bones, but then, all men were in love with Veronica. Old beaux of hers used to drop by the coatroom, visiting us, paying Veronica tribute, which she received, not in the least impressed, as only her due.

"Vino!" squealed Veronica, reaching for the glass with a long, languid arm. "Charlotte, it's about time!"

Veronica's voice—oh, Veronica's voice held the kind of accent that could be heard only in Boston and nowhere else in America. When I was a child, I used to pretend it was British, though of course I had it wrong. Veronica was a Bostonian, Radcliffe class of '63.

In the coatroom there were two chairs behind the podium, one for Veronica and one for me. I sat down and we got to work on our latest project, which was renaming Marlon Brando's numerous legitimate and illegitimate children. There were eleven of them, or maybe fourteen, depending on what source you read.

I'd fallen in love with Marlon Brando—if *love* is not too elevated a word—after Veronica had taken me to see *A Streetcar Named Desire* at the Brattle Theatre. There he was in moody black-and-white close-up, peeling off his bowling jacket and moistening his lips, his face alluringly angelic and childlike above the husky build below.

I understood, immediately, that Marlon Brando was not the kind of man for whom you would buy a cashmere sweater from the Andover Shop; Marlon Brando was for other things.

We left the theatre and Veronica, whirling across Brattle Street with her light, lovely steps, more a young girl's steps than an older woman's, exclaimed, "My God, but I'd forgotten. Marlon is glorious, no? Such divine animal brutishness!" Then, in an altogether different tone of voice, she added, "This is a quality in short supply in the men of Cambridge, Mass."

Coming up with new names for people was nothing new for Veronica and me. I was "Cordelia" and my mother "Celeste." Veronica gave herself an Italian name: "Rafaella." Giving people fake names came in handy, because it meant that we could sit out in the open in Harvard Square— splitting a chocolate-apricot layer cake at the Window Shop, drinking vino in the olive-green leather banquettes at Harvest—gossiping about people and no one would guess who we were talking about.

We wrote out the new fake names of Marlon Brando's children in a red felt pen on the back of one of the menus. *Isaac Vendetta Brando. Romeo Paradiso Brando. Gina Valentina Brando.* Veronica had extraordinary handwriting—strong and slashing, like a sword. Among her friends, she was famous for her letters, which she wrote out on French stationery, and in which she spared the recipient no candid word.

After we came up with the names, we gave the children identities.

"Giulietta Brando," I said. "What's her backstory? I say he had her before *Streetcar.*"

"Yes," said Veronica. "The mother worked in a used bookstore in the Village, I think. Brunette pageboy, cat-eye glasses . . ."

"But of course. Marlon only ever went for brunettes." I sighed.

Jotting notes on the back of another menu, Veronica continued. "He went into the bookstore looking for books on acting, on Stanislavski, you understand. It was love at first sight."

"For him or for her?"

"For *her*. She said, 'I'm not going to have an abortion. I'm going to have your baby, Marlon. I'm going to raise this baby, *Giulietta,* in the Village.' It was a beatnik childhood. Marlon went off to LA, he sold out to the movies, he never visited."

Sometimes customers helped us name the Brando children. One night, we agreed that one of the daughters should be named Theodora, but we couldn't come up with the right middle name. A couple, reeling down the staircase and obviously in love, came and got their coats. Veronica sized them up by saying, "*Buona sera!* And what did *you* two drink for dinner?"

"Cassis," answered the man without the slightest hesitation. "Cassis and soda."

"With raspberries on top," added the woman as Veronica helped her into her coat.

"Cassis!" Veronica exclaimed. "Cassis, Charlotte—I mean, *Cordelia*—write that down immediately, don't you dare forget it."

"What?"

"Cordelia, now you are usually much more swift on the uptake. Cassis! Write it down. Theodora Cassis! That's it. Theodora Cassis Brando. Divine, perfect, finished, done, who wouldn't want to be named Theodora Cassis?" Veronica turned on the woman—she and her husband were just standing there staring at us. "Wouldn't *you* like to be named Theodora Cassis?"

"We're renaming Marlon Brando's children," I said by way of casual explanation.

"We've been at it for months," said Veronica. "Come back next year this time, why don't you? We might still be at it, whittled down to the bone, quite obliterated by all our hard work, the two of us."

This was when we had those divine Parmesan-fried lamb chops on the menu, and on Sunday nights in the coatroom with Veronica I always ordered them. Veronica, preferring, on the whole, vino to food, didn't eat things like lamb chops. I never saw her order an entree. But she did like my mother's roasted-sweet-red-pepper soup, which all the grown-ups adored and was even the favorite dish of Julia Child whenever she dined at the Pudding.

I didn't quite see what the fuss was about that soup, myself. I preferred tastes that were obvious and offered up their pleasures without complication: red meat, milk chocolate. But I did note the fact that even Veronica, usually so indifferent to food, couldn't resist this particular soup. Could it be that its deep flavors—the bitter under-taste of the red peppers—held some voluptuous secret that only the grown-ups could appreciate?

Many of the waiters and bartenders on the staff shared

our Marlon Brando obsession. Veronica and I used to keep a ragged copy of *Streetcar* in the coatroom, and the sight of Brando bare-chested on the cover produced such giddiness in the staff ("Charlotte, my dear! What ever are you reading? Oh, *Streetcar*. My favorite!") that Veronica finally wrote on a sticky note *This is a yellow T-shirt* and put it on Brando's chest.

There was even one waiter who, at the end of the night after the customers had gone, would change out of his uniform and stand there in his boxer shorts only to quote Blanche DuBois from memory. "And I'll be buried at sea sewn up in a clean white sack and dropped overboard—at noon—in the blaze of summer—and into an ocean as blue as my first lover's eyes!"

I would play along; I would snap my fingers and say, "From eating an unwashed grape!"

"Exactly," said the waiter, impressed by my youthful knowledge. "Oh, Stella, Stella for star!"

"Do runway," commanded Veronica, and when Veronica commanded something, you listened. She combined the severity of a governess with the liquid glamour of a movie star. "Do runway" meant that she wanted the waiter to try on a piece of her clothing. In this case, it was a black velvet brocade opera coat, which, in spite of its being Italian, Veronica had decided was too big for her. She bought things purely on impulse at Filene's Basement and that was the fun of it. She gave the waiter the coat; he shimmied around in it, doing Blanche, stalking the long corridor that ran from the restrooms to the coatroom, for all the world as if it were a real runway.

"Calma, calma!" said Veronica, taking the coat away from him; Veronica would indulge people but *only up to a point.* Even with the gay guys, she was a flirt, deft in the feminine arts of delight and withdrawal. All winter long I watched her, her and her black velvet dresses, the long rhinestone earrings that brushed her swan's neck, the neck that could only belong to an Avedon model. She had a new lover that winter and was wearing a new perfume. It was vanilla, she told me, but unlike anything so sweet as the flavor I identified in my mother's desserts. It was vanilla, but dangerous. Maybe on Veronica it was more like the Italian word for vanilla, darker, dreamier: *vaniglia.*

During this period, a man named Giancarlo was the wine steward. Actually, his real name wasn't Giancarlo, it was John, but Veronica called him Giancarlo to his face, and I imitated her. He was a small, plump-bellied man with a petulant expression, who, no matter what he was wearing, always looked like he should have been stuffed into a red velvet smoking jacket. It was with Giancarlo's histrionic tantrums in mind that my mother had threatened to post a

sign in the kitchen reading PLEASE DON'T SPEAK TO THE
WAITERS UNTIL THEY HAVE TAKEN THEIR MEDICATIONS.

One night, Giancarlo propped his chin on the podium of
the coatroom and said, "Let me tell you a little anecdote
about Ayn Rand. I think it may shed some light on this great
hungry longing of yours for dear Marlon."

"Go ahead," I said.

"All right. Some journalist once asked Ayn Rand, 'Why
is the sex in your books so violent?' and what do you think
she said?"

"What?"

"Wishful thinking."

When I used to do the coatroom with Veronica,
the prospect of the lightening days at the end of
the winter was for me tinged with sorrow. Because when
the warm weather came and people were no longer wearing heavy coats, the solace of our Sunday night routine—
the enchanted intimacy between us—would be broken.
And also, I could never count on Veronica to stay in Cambridge for long. She was a world traveler. She'd jet off to
Rome or Budapest or London, leaving behind cryptic messages on her answering machine: "*Buongiorno.* Be warned:
I'm not returning calls these days. Leave a message if you

must." Or sometimes she simply sang into the machine before it beeped, old folky-type songs in a sweetly wavering soprano.

And so now, walking down Holyoke Street alone, I passed seersucker, not tweed, in the windows of the Andover Shop. The lilacs were out on Brattle Street again, and fiddlehead ferns appeared on the menu for their brief, sweet, green spell before vanishing altogether for another whole year.

By this time, when I was in the seventh grade, I should have been wearing a bra. But somehow, I wasn't. My mother, whose succulent Joy-perfumed cleavage was a great part of her feminine identity in the world, never mentioned the subject to me. Certainly we never had, were never going to have, *the talk*.

That spring I had a favorite dress, bought from a store on Mass Ave that sold children's fashions imported from Paris. It was black poplin scattered with a pattern of tight little cherries, barely ripe, and had a Peter Pan collar, dirndl skirt, and a row of plastic buttons in the shape of cherries down the front. Painted cherries and plastic cherries, cherries and more cherries—my beloved cherry dress. But then month by month, week by week, bit by bit, the buttons stretched across my budding chest: it looked as if I was going to inherit my mother's extravagant figure after all.

Then one day at recess, a luminous spring afternoon, I raised my arms, and *rip!* Two of the buttons burst, the ones right across my chest. My breasts emerged out of shaken cherries and hung unsheathed, two lonesome white bells in April air.

That was the last of the cherry dress. And I did, after that, get a bra. (And soon after that, highlights, restoring my ashy hair to its childhood gold.) But in the dressing room, being fitted for one by some strange woman snapping open a tape measure at my untouched skin, I cried. I cried with my whole body, and in a way I would go on to cry on several other occasions in my life, when you know that you are leaving someone, or something, forever.

That was in the spring. And by the time it was winter and Veronica was back in Cambridge doing the coatroom on Sunday nights again, all of my dresses, not just that black velvet one, came from the grown-ups' department.

Eleven

DOVER
SOLE

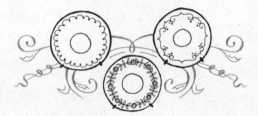

When I was fourteen, my father lost his longtime studio above the train tracks in Waltham. Over the years, I had noticed that the building itself was changing. The landlord had raised the rent, forcing many of the artists to move out. Now it was only subsidized housewives who could afford the rent, painting fruit still lifes in the afternoon before they picked up their children from school. They turned the drafty building where mice had scurried in the hallways and dust had hung thick from the rafters into a civilized place. They kept bottles of peppermint soap and rolls of paper towels in the bathroom, swept the floor, and called the exterminator to report mouse sightings. Sometimes they knocked on my father's door, asking if he wanted to try some pâté they had picked up at the grocery store. My father would taste the pâté, but he disliked what they had done to the building; and soon he, too, could no longer afford the rent and had to find someplace else to go.

For a time, after getting kicked out of a girlfriend's house, he lived in a studio in downtown Boston, not far from Chinatown. He shared it with a number of other artists, but he was the only one who slept there, on a rust-colored sleeping bag with a busted zipper flung on the dusty floor. When I visited him there, I could see holes in the wall, and I wondered if rats lurked behind the cobwebs.

"What do you think of that sofa?" my father asked me, pointing. "Isn't it great? It's called a fainting couch."

I did like the sofa: moss green velvet, curved low to the ground. I liked the name, too: *a fainting couch*. It was the only piece of furniture in the room, and made a very dramatic statement.

"Hey, Luu-Luu, cut it out."

A Persian cat was scratching the fainting couch. Rips already ran up and down the sides.

"If you see another cat around here, that's Nixon," he said. "At least he catches the mice sometimes. *She's* just useless."

Luu-Luu clawed the couch as my father lit another cigarette.

"I like it here," he said. Then, his face brightening up as if he had a secret, "Hey, Char, you know what you can see from the window?"

"What?"

My father pointed out the long window. This was during the years of the Big Dig construction project, and much of the city of Boston was torn up and in chaos. But in the distance, my father had something he wanted to show me.

"Elmo!" he announced.

"Elmo?"

"Oh, I forgot, we never made you watch *Sesame Street* or any of that crap. Look, Char, see that big red monster on top of the Children's Museum? Parents think that thing is wholesome? Christ. I think it's demonic. When it's windy out, it moves, and I always say, 'Look! Elmo's drunk again!'"

I looked, and there, as promised, was the enormous Elmo mounted on top of the Children's Museum, his shaggy red fur waving just slightly in the breeze, black button eyes dilated. My father got it absolutely right: demonic.

My father laughed, his deep belly laugh.

"You know what Veronica says about the Children's Museum?"

"What, Char?"

"She says, 'If I were a child today, I feel confident that I would hate being taken to the Children's Museum.'"

My father and I howled, for it went without saying that I hated things like going to the Children's Museum, too. I had only ever gone there on field trips, which were lonesome for me; I always sat next to the teacher on the bus. Actually, it was on one of these field trips—the day my sixth grade class went to an ice-skating rink—that I, sitting by myself on the bench and watching my peers glide by on the ice, had one of those melancholy forebodings people have sometimes that ring of absolute truth: *all of the grown-ups are going to die.* And for a split second, I had a vague, shivery premonition of just how lonely my twenties would be.

We left the studio and went out to eat in Chinatown with a friend of my father's. I could always count on him to produce new people, new characters. This time it was a beautiful, coltish young woman with long, dark, Victorian hair and something tragic in her eyes, and I figured my father must have been photographing her. We ordered plenty of food, my father trying to convince the waiter to get us some of the more alluring dishes he saw the Chinese families eating. His last girlfriend was Chinese and a real asset whenever we ordered food in Chinatown. My father, without her, was desperate not to miss out on some nameless treasure. Somehow, without a word of Chinese, he always succeeded in winning over the waiter—not by being pushy, for he was not a pushy man, but just by being respectful and curious, by conveying a warm and casual appreciation of the cuisine and the culture.

The food arrived, sizzling full-flavored dish after sizzling full-flavored dish. We all dug in, without the slightest self-consciousness. The conversation flitted over a number of subjects, only to land on the avant-garde filmmaker Stan Brakhage. One time, in New York City, my father took me to see a film of his about what happened to dead people's body parts.

"Oh, God," I said, remembering; images from the film, buried for years, had come back to me. "That movie was gross."

"There was nothing gross about it, Char," said my father, "but have it your way; I can't stop you. I thought it was so interesting getting to see all the things that might hap-pen to your body after you're gone. You should become an organ donor, Char, when you get your license. I am; that's just about the one thing I believe in." My father took an-other helping of bird's nest soup, a big smile on his face. "I'm telling you, Char. I can't wait until I'm dead."

Around this time I found, while rooting through milk crates during our latest move, a stack of reviews and arti-cles about the Pudding from back when my father was still the head chef. I was careful not to rip the crackly paper, and I read the words in faded ink. In one of the articles, the reporter mentioned my father bringing Dover sole home for me at the end of the night. "My daughter is going to love this." I tried to picture my father standing over my high chair, scooping pieces of Dover sole onto my pink tin tray, but the image felt remote to me by now. It was all so long ago.

*S*ince leaving Dudley Road, we had lived in a number of different apartments, almost always near the Cambridge-Somerville line, for years. We always rented, and would move when leases ran out, or when, as was so often the case, the rent was raised. But then one afternoon my mother came home from the restaurant and told me as she was pulling off her apron, "We're moving. Next month."

"Oh."

"But it's different now: we're *buying.*"

"Where? Did you find a house?"

"Oh, no," she said. "Just upstairs."

My mother, it turned out, had toured a condo on the third floor of the building where we were living at the time, decided that the sunshine would be marvelous for her pink geraniums, and agreed to buy it. We moved on schedule a month later, just the two of us. Benjamin was at this point living in Northern California. "Why bother with movers," she said, "when it's only upstairs?" The building was a red-brick Victorian schoolhouse that had been converted into

condominiums, and the ceilings were high and the oak staircase broad and seemingly endless. For two days, we lugged
everything we owned up the stairs to our new home. At
night, I fell asleep to the sound of my mother hammering
hooks to hang the plates on the wall.

She devoted herself to the decoration of the condo.
Every morning, she clawed the carpet out with her bare
hands, bit by bit, before she went into the restaurant. Then
she hired a painter to dapple pink peonies and silver-leaf
polka dots on the floor and ribbons on the walls. She put
lavender porcelain doorknobs on my armoire, even though
I said the old knobs suited me just fine, and painted the armoire itself a gray called Kid Glove and the walls of my bedroom a pink called Degas. There was not a splotch of white
paint anywhere in the condo. Some mornings I awoke to the
sounds of hammers pounding and ladders scraping. Once
I drifted into the living room in my flannel nightgown only
to see a bare-chested stranger standing on a ladder, paint-
brush in hand.

"Charlotte," my mother said, click-clacking out of the
kitchen on her stilettos, "meet my friend Danny."

"Hello, Danny," I said in my little-girl voice, stifling a yawn.

"Danny is my friend. And he's going to paint the walls
Maiden Sunrise. What do you think?"

"Wonderful," I said, rubbing my eyes.

Then she rooted through the boxes tumbled on the floor till she found the one she was looking for. "Aren't these cunning?" she said, taking mother-of-pearl forks out of sheets of tissue paper. "Won't they be perfect for shrimp cocktail?"

"That would make a good appetizer," I told her. "I think people would order it."

"At home!" she said. "I'm going to make shrimp cocktail at home, just you wait."

A couple of years after we had moved into the condo, when the living-room walls had become Maiden Sunrise and Confetti and Amethyst Phlox and Macaroon, an editor from *Boston Magazine* asked my mother if they could photograph the condo for their upcoming style-at-home issue. "I'm sorry, Charlotte," she told me, weaving between the empty paint cans in the hallway. "It's going to be a little bit chaotic here until we finish with this photo shoot."

It was then before Christmas. On Christmas morning, when I opened my presents underneath the topiary tree my mother had decked with her costume jewelry, she told me, "Now, about the bathrobe. Oh, it's *beautiful* cotton, isn't it? But I really only bought it for the photo shoot." It was white terry cloth embroidered with pink satin hearts around the collar. I loved it, but my mother took it away in case the photographer wanted to feature it in the photo shoot.

She wanted to hang the bathrobe off the porcelain hooks she planned to drill into my wall, if only she had the time: "You can't imagine the pressure I'm under."

One day after school, I stepped into the condo and heard tinkling female voices in the living room. My mother had gotten all the ladders out of the hallway and flicked on the rose-shaded lamps. I smelled something in the kitchen—something rich and lingering. It must have been food.

"Charlotte," my mother called from the living room, "help yourself to some of the chicken soup I made. It's delicious."

"Absolutely delicious," the other woman said.

"Charlotte, come meet my friend Emily."

Emily, the Features editor for *Boston Magazine*, had come to the condo to interview my mother. "Wonderful," she said, shaking my hand. "Now I can ask you questions, too."

I sat down on one of the white wrought-iron chairs. My mother had brought out one of our cake stands, the pink-check porcelain one, and piled the tiers with chocolate-dipped strawberries and pistachio biscotti.

"So," Emily said, "I take it you like pink, too."

"Pink lightbulbs are terrible for your eyes," I said, reaching for a biscotto, "but they're wonderful for the complexion."

Emily laughed. Then she said, "So tell me. Which table do you guys eat dinner at? I was wondering about that."

A-1, I wanted to say, thinking of the table at the Pudding where we ate so many of our meals.

"Oh," I said after a pause. "The truth is, Emily, we're very fond of all the tables."

The magazine came out that April. Our condo looked magnificent: the black-and-white floors sparkled, the vases of peonies delivered by Serge the florist lined the windows, and the pink lightbulbs made the living room glow like the inside of a bottle of grenadine. "In Cambridge, Hughes became a serial renter," Emily wrote, "moving a dozen times in eight years." It was then that I realized I had never kept track of the number myself.

Years later, when I went away to college, my mother ended up selling that condo. We moved again, this time to the house my mother lives in now. For months and months, the condo languished on the market, its candy-slicked painted surfaces and gold-leaf embellishments too extreme a statement for most people's tastes. Then, one day just as she was beginning to despair that she'd have to whitewash the condo in order to sell it, my mother at long last found a buyer. The catch? The buyer was color-blind. All colors read to him, he assured the Realtor, as one color only: "a soft," he said, "gentle gray."

But my mother's dream house would not have been that

condo, or even the house she went on to buy later on; it would have been, always and forever, the farmhouse she'd left behind on Dudley Road. Sometimes, never in the dead of the winter, but in the spring and the summer when green things were growing and memories stirring, my mother and I would drive out to Bedford, to the site where the farm-house had been before the developer bought up the land. The first time we finally saw it after all of those years, I remember thinking that the cluster of condominiums looked like a housing complex named "Fern Court" or "Ivy Circle." It might have been anywhere in the entire country, not necessarily New England. Bulldozers had long since smashed several of our neighbors' homes to the ground, and in their place we saw one-sized houses with fresh coats of tan paint and fuzzy welcoming mats on the stone stoops underneath the doors.

We went and toured our old house, the only one still standing. Since it was now the information center for prospective buyers, a row of shelves in my former bedroom displayed swatches of carpeting and wallpaper for people to choose from. Someone had whitewashed the raspberry walls and replaced the mint green floors with wall-to-wall carpeting.

"I hate wallpaper," my mother whispered to me. "*And* carpeting. What is that color, anyway, *taupe? Natural?*"

In the bathroom, she sniffed the cluster of poppies in a white plastic vase on the sink.

"Fake," she said. "Thought so."

After we left, I tried to picture the farmhouse, what it had been like when I was a little girl. I remembered the rickety swing set and the rose and blue wax drizzled on the dining-room table, the pink tin tray my mother had served me poached eggs on when I was sick. I remembered, suddenly, the pink-and-green Shetland sweater she used to wear underneath her aprons every day.

But I remembered also my father's darkroom, and how, getting home from the Pudding, he would disappear into its private, silvery depths. I remembered the stench of the photo chemicals floating out of that darkroom, and how they tinged with something bitter and metallic the more tender smells I associated with the yellow kitchen: those of bubbling chocolate and cinnamon, brioche and bacon.

In the end, my brother and I will inherit boxes of my father's photographs—one box labeled in my father's elegant hand *Benjamin* and the other *Charlotte*. I will brush the dust off the lid; open the box. In it, I will find some of the oldest of my father's photographs, most of them taken at Dudley Road and showing one unifying obsession—brooms. Brooms, enrobed, held captive in gelatin molds of translucent silver light. Brooms printed not only on rice paper but on the backs of chewing-gum wrappers and on the papers of packages of Camel cigarettes. Brooms tickling the floor, brooms afloat in the air. Brooms dipped in silver leaf, brooms without silver leaf. Brooms, brooms, brooms.

Are they all that remain, these lonesome brooms, of my father's hours in that darkroom; of Dudley Road itself; of our childhoods?

Now, back in the car, I looked at my mother sitting next to me in the driver's seat, the violet frames of her sunglasses casting shadows on her face at the voluptuous end of a summer's afternoon.

And then she said, "I forgot, we never went to the pond."

A pond, down the road from the farmhouse, came back to me. We had walked there in the winter, my mother and Benjamin and I, after the cups of cocoa that were always so delicious and made velvety with heavy cream.

"I tried to teach you to ice-skate once, remember?"

The pond blurred to blue and white. It might have been any pond, anywhere. I remembered so many different things, but I did not remember ice skates.

"I *guess*."

We drove on, the farm stands and the country roads receding from view.

I have just remembered what I had forgotten: that the first time I went back to Dudley Road was not in the company of my mother but my father. He drove me out there one day. I think it must have been a Sunday; I think, *I imagine,* it must have been the month of May. I could only have been seven or eight years old at the time. We walked and walked, my father and I, deep into the thickening woods. My father had with him a fragile straw basket. He was prowling the crannies of the woods for mushrooms, trumpets of death. But instead of mushrooms we found a lady's slipper. Just one, that day, ravished at the husk of a great big tree. Pink and wet, dangerous and endangered, unlike the more modest, less troubling British flowers that used to be in my mother's garden, unlike any flower I had ever seen.

Lady's slippers were then thought to be extinct, and in Massachusetts in those days it was illegal to pick them. My father, whose mind was encyclopedic, knew this; my father knew everything.

But, "Oh, the hell with that, Char," he said, and now, now I can think back through the years and picture my father's body, shrouded in black, bent at the pink wings of the lady's slipper, lifting her sleepy green stem out of the earth, handing her to me, a beautiful, poisoned apple.

My father had long, deft fingers, an artist's hands; she would not have suffered.

I took the lady's slipper back to my father's studio that day. Then I took her home with me and she was mine until she died.

Twelve

ON
LEMON ICE

I don't know why I hired him," my mother said. "It must have been the tattoo."

Gus was our latest head chef. He was six feet five, and my mother said he was as wide as the cold room. Beneath his shaved head, a tattoo was printed on the nape of his neck. CAN'T STOP WON'T STOP it read in thick black letters.

"It seemed like a good idea at the time," she said. "With a message like that tattooed on his flesh, I didn't think he'd dare take any sick days."

By the time Gus worked at the Pudding, I spent hardly any time in the kitchen anymore. I only stepped through the black-painted double doors to grab a brownie the kitchen had set out for staff lunch or, more often, to thank the chefs for dinner at the end of the night. In my gold lamé slippers and pert pink cocktail dresses, I would peer over the metal shelf at the chefs behind the line, in their blood-spotted whites and dank, dripping bandannas. Chefs still wore bandannas then, when I was in my teens, although I cannot recall if they still smoked behind the line, or if the ban on smoking in restaurants had already happened.

Before he had arrived at the Pudding, it was rumored that Gus had spent some time in a New York state prison. My mother assumed the charges had involved drugs, or gangs, or both; in any case, he could do wonders with red snapper, and she said he was the most talented head chef we had employed since my father had left the restaurant, and us, years ago. Gus was the one who started calling my mother "Patton in Pumps," because she had no illusions about life behind the line: it was a battle, and you had to lead your troops.

The rest of the Pudding mystified him. He called the waiters "Tinkerbells," as in "Flounce back to your table, Tinkerbell, and tell the poor suckers *everything* has salt." Once, watching the Krokodiloes perform one of their fifties doo-wop numbers during Sunday brunch, he said, "Man, they really take the rock *out* of rock and roll." He despised above all the Hasty Pudding Club members, who mixed martinis with a deathly seriousness over the pool table in the first-floor Members' Lounge and had first names like Chip and Grayson and Bridge. "Love to run into one of *them* in a jail cell," he said.

I liked Gus as I had liked few of the recent chefs; he reminded me of the fringy, dissolute, yet somehow endearing kitchen personalities of my childhood. "Hey, Shorty," he asked me, "what's your deal, anyway? Did you get beat up a lot on the playground? Did fags used to pack sprigs of parsley in your lunch box?" Sometimes when he passed my table, he glanced at my plate and said, "Foie gras. Foie gras on a fucking school night." But he approved of my pink wardrobe, and one time he tried on my pink rain slicker with the rhinestone buttons; it fit him more like a bolero. He wore it out on the streets of Harvard Square. "This isn't campy, Shorty, you know that," he told me. "It's just that this is one cool look."

My mother had insisted that Gus was "honestly a cream puff," meaning that under the tough exterior he was very tenderhearted. He talked to himself behind the line; once I heard him say, as he pounded Parmesan bread crumbs onto a lamb chop, "Tonight I'm either going to get into a fight or get laid. I'm not very good at either." He also scanned the menu for typos, exclaiming, "*Fennel* with one *n*, can you believe this shit?" His cuisine struck me as delicate, for the Pudding, which had always been known for its delicious but none-too-daring gentleman's club cuisine, the richer, the better. Gus's dishes included dabs of steak tartare placed on top of thinly peeled cucumbers and studded with quail eggs; poached sea bass on top of a scoop of asparagus puree;

potatoes mousseline whipped so smooth you could not detect even the flecks of pepper.

Whether Gus had cleaned up from the drugs we never knew, but he was an alcoholic. When he was sober, he tried to drink grenadine straight from the bottle, as I had underneath the bar when I was a little girl, because he thought that all the sugar would reduce his cravings. "No way will I put this in a glass," he told the bartenders. "Then you'd deck it out with cherries and shit, like one of Shorty's drinks over there, and I'd think you had funny ideas about me." But the staff teased him about the deep pink bottles that said ROSE'S GRENADINE in swirly letters, and so he emptied beer bottles and filled them with the grenadine instead. Everyone suspected he guzzled the beer himself, in the bathroom. He left the bottles on the butcher block, and sometimes during the eight o'clock rush a cook tipped one of them over and then the pink liquid would ooze onto the wood.

But after a three-day bender one weekend, during which no one could find him, my mother fired her latest and most gifted head chef.

"It was the timing, Gus," she told him. "No head chef ever bails on a Saturday night."

After that, Gus came back to the restaurant sometimes to visit my mother, but only when he was sober. He sat down across from her at A-1, slinging his leather jacket over the gilded back of the chair. "Please stay for lunch," she said every time. "We'd love, love, love to have you." The front of the house had to settle for staff lunch and I had to order off the menu, but chefs and former chefs got special samples: thumb-sized dabs of pâté; a new entree, duck breast with fingerling potatoes and artichokes, not yet on the menu; chocolate éclairs whipped up that morning in the pastry station, just for the fun of it. "You're the real talent, Gus," my mother said at the end of the meal, smacking one of her Coco Pink kisses on his cheek.

After a while, Gus didn't stop by for lunch anymore; he didn't even come back for the staff Christmas parties in the Club Bar. And it seems to me now that Gus was the last truly colorful figure who worked in the kitchen. It was right around the time he worked at the Pudding that the entire restaurant business at large began to change. Fashionable restaurants with aggressive haute cuisine were springing up in Boston, formerly a baked-beans-and-cod town. Chefs were just starting to get their own television shows, a development that would have been laughable in my childhood, when the chefs I knew were hardly fit to be seen in public, let alone on television. Surveying the new generation of more career-oriented chefs, my mother said, "What a pity. It used to be that one went into the restaurant business to get away from all of the people who wanted to be doctors and lawyers. Now, who knew? All of the people who used to become doctors and lawyers now want to be chefs! It's spoiling the business, if you ask me."

*E*very spring, my mother gave a special dinner for our investors. The dinners had a reliable rhythm to them, coming to Cambridge once a year like the Head of the Charles and being conducted with some of the same stately seriousness. The menu never varied that much, and, adding to the collegiate flavor of the evening, since so many of our investors were Harvard men, the dinners were held not upstairs in the dining room but downstairs in the Club Bar.

After the entree had been served, a comfortable hush settled over the room. The investors' bellies, bloated from my mother's fava-bean soup with roasted pecans and crème fraîche, strained the fabric of their tuxedos. The wives fared better at the end of these meals, having opted for poached salmon instead of veal chops. The private-party staff cleared away the main courses, and now the men waited—sleeves rolled up and heirloom cuff links tossed on bread plates—for cups of coffee. They gestured to the waiters to fill their wineglasses so they could give toasts.

We depended on the investors. They had helped to start the restaurant, and they helped to keep it in business. We owed them VIP tables, air kisses, and elaborate desserts. We slipped off the barstools to make room for them, remembered how much horseradish they liked in their Bloody Marys, and patted their arms and assured them that they would *love* the escargots appetizer, if only they would try it.

"I want to tell you," our head investor said now, "none of this wonderful night would have been possible without two women, yes, two wonderful women . . ."

He paused. Mary-Catherine was there, waiting, but my mother had not yet appeared. Everyone applauded, but my mother did not appear. Then, as the applause petered out, one of the investors raised his wineglass to me, and the burgundy dregs plopped on his matching bow tie. "Charlotte," he said, "Charlotte, why don't you stand up for us? Come on, represent your mother."

The applause mounted again as I stood up from my seat. "Thank you," I said. "Thank you all for coming."

"What did I tell you? She's every bit as pretty as her mother."

Then the waiters served the dessert: Sicilian lemon pound cake on a bed of lemon ice. Propped on top of each slice were marzipan party hats sprinkled with pink dots, and a lit candle stuck out of each party hat. My mother had hand-squeezed the lemons for the ices, beat the batter for the pound cakes, and hand-molded the party hats. She had been at the restaurant since three o'clock in the morning. Now she was hiding—I suspected—in the rickety, urine-sprayed stall in the kitchen, trying to avoid the toasts. For all that she was such a flamboyant personality, she hated the formality of these evenings; she hated having any kind of tribute paid to her. It was, in part, a question of "front room vs. kitchen." The kitchen was where she belonged.

"I hope I don't get caught," I could hear her saying to the staff. "I always get caught."

In any event, it was a beautiful dessert. Sicilian lemon pound cake had been on the menu when I was a little girl, and I had missed it. Then I looked around the Club Bar at other people's plates: the cakes had already crumbled, the party hats had split in half, and the candles floated in the yellow puddles. I wished that the party hat were a real party hat. I wished it were made out of paper and sequins instead of marzipan and pink food dye. Then I would slip it in my pink beaded clutch, like I did other keepsakes: menus, dance cards, roses.

Already I was collecting a trail of bread crumbs that might lead me, one day, back to the Pudding once it was gone. But it was hard to do this. The art of fine dining is a cruelly ephemeral one. What perishes faster than the labors of the kitchen?

She had tough hands, my mother. Tough enough to withstand labors of the kitchen. In the course of a single day, her hands lifted copper pots, cracked walnut shells, and hollowed out chicken guts. But that was in the kitchen. At home, preparing to go back to the restaurant to hold court in the dining room at night, these same hands dabbed Joy perfume on her temples, behind the wisps of blond hair that were, in marked contrast to her calloused hands, as angelically fine as a baby's.

But right around this time, the time of this investor dinner, something had started happening to my mother's hands—something rather ominous. She was shedding her nails. They snapped, like asparagus tips, one by one. "I've used my hands," she said. "That's why." And then, in wonderment, she would survey the cracked tips, the swollen knuckles, in front of her, as if to ask where had all those years of hard work gone, and what did she have to show for them.

The years when I was a teenager—the mid- to late nineties—happened to coincide with the most vibrant years of business at the Pudding, when the massive

dining room was full of customers on any given night. Reservations for holiday dinners, with special menus featuring
all of the most decadent ingredients, sold out long in ad-
vance. Come the first promise of warm weather, sometime
after the ice on the Charles had thawed but before the lilacs
were out, my mother started planting her window boxes on
the herb-garden terrace. For Easter brunch, there would be
hyacinths, pink and white as well as the more famous purple. By Harvard graduation, when the Pudding regularly did
four hundred–plus customers, there would be roses—pink,
salmon, golden, cream, but never red, for my mother had an
aversion to flowers in that brassy, boastful color. She favored
the gentle palette and loose, feminine profusion of an English garden, and it was there, in such a setting cradled high
above the streets of Harvard Square, where customers dined
in large numbers. For a certain era in Cambridge, that terrace was *the* place to be.

Of course, by the nineties the Pudding was no longer
the only glamorous dining destination in the Square, and
Boston at large was beginning to produce its first batch of
"celebrity" chefs. One of these, it was rumored, made his
employees address him as "Oui, Chef," even though, my
mother was quick to point out, he came from New Jersey.
It looked like the restaurant business was turning into the

kind of operation where fame could be found and fortunes made. But then at that time, people were making
fortunes all over the place and in all different fields. No
doubt this allowed them to splurge on meals at restaurants
like the Pudding, boosting our business. But this culture of
fast fortunes—easy business opportunities—didn't always
change things for the better.

Harvard Square when I was a child had its share of lov-
able dumps: Elsie's and its pastrami sandwiches, Bailey's
and its butterscotch sundaes, and, most famously, The Tasty,
which was a neighborhood favorite not so much for food
as for the scruffy camaraderie at its dinky yellow linoleum
counter. It was at that counter that Harvard professors
might mingle with homeless people over fried-egg sandwiches, or maybe a plate of french fries.

The year I was sixteen, Cambridge Savings Bank, which
was the landlord of both The Tasty and the old-time German restaurant the Wursthaus, realized that they could
make much more money renting space to chain stores.
After a series of fruitless protests from the community, they
replaced those two institutions with an Abercrombie &
Fitch and a Pacific Sunwear. And so, here in Harvard Square,
land of the life of the mind, sprang up enormous soft-porn
billboards of ripped young men hawking preripped Aber-

crombie jeans. Hawaiian shirts and California-dreaming
sundresses gleamed out of the windows of what had once
been the Wursthaus, where Nabokov in his letters wrote of
meeting Edmund Wilson for lunch in the fifties.

The palette, the palette was the thing; the palette was the
difference. The reason I flinched, at once, from the colors
of the items in the Pacific Sunwear window was the same
reason my mother flinched from red roses: they were too
one-note, too bold. Cambridge, being the ultimate preppy
town, had always been a place of dim colors and deep tex-
tures. Had Cambridge been a fabric, it would have been
Shetland wool. Had it been a smell, it would have been one
of those old-time pipe tobaccos, as offered at Leavitt &
Peirce: Black Coffee or Cherry Cavendish, Dark Honey or
Amaretto.

After The Tasty closed, it wasn't long before the Coop
changed hands, too. Harvard agreed to sell the Coop's
bookstore to Barnes & Noble, provided they didn't change
the name on the sign, and indeed, people still spoke of
it as "the Coop." From the outside it looked the same, but
inside I felt the difference, as I could taste the difference
between the roasted capons we served at the Pudding
and fast-food chicken tenders. The white walls twinkled
and the railings of the staircase looked like they were made
out of plastic. Tourists did not know that the Coop had

been, above all, shabby, that one afternoon in its final days, a high school friend of mine had tried to take a picture of the Square through one of the windows and couldn't, because of all the dust. "That is one filthy window," he had said; it had been, once.

Thirteen

CABANA
BOYS

*M*eanwhile, cloistered in the gilded Victorian rooms of 10 Holyoke Street, we went on as though nothing had changed. The same year The Tasty closed, my mother threw me a lavish Sweet Sixteen birthday party downstairs in the Club Bar. The party took place in the middle of a snowstorm, making the gracious red-walled room as cozy as the hot center of a jam tart. There were three cakes (chocolate dacquoise, coconut-lemon cream, and strawberry-mascarpone) all with shapely, fluted, pale green letters pressed into them reading *Happy Sweet Sixteen, Charlotte*. I myself must have brought to mind a pastry that night, wearing a confection of fluffy almond-colored tulle.

The dress, whose strapless sweetheart neckline and sweeping skirt recalled, I hoped, the famous white lilac dress Elizabeth Taylor wore in the ballroom of *A Place in the Sun*, also made me think of something my mother would have worn. Recently, I had found some pictures of my mother wearing a fluffy white dress and lavender-dyed dancing pumps to a ball she and Mary-Catherine had gone to at Harvard, and it surprised me to notice that her taste was rather less flashy now. Her color palette, for one thing, had mellowed. Gone were those rich, saturated parma violets and crocodile greens; now my mother wore subtle seafoams and terra-cottas, champagnes and silvers. The hourglass silhouette, however, remained intact.

It was right around the time of my Sweet Sixteen party that I began shopping vintage. When I was in high school, dresses from the romantic era of "the New Look" were still easily available and not nearly as expensive as they are today. In no time, I collected a marvelous assortment of them.

The first piece of vintage clothing I ever bought was a pink satin cocktail dress starred all over with little gold dots, which, as people often remarked whenever I wore it in the dining room, matched the decor of the restaurant. I think it was only when I first stood in front of the dressing-room mirror in that dress that I realized I had inherited my mother's figure after all and that it might be fun to show it off. And I did. I *loved* my waist. I *loved* my stomach. I loved the dip and curve of it beneath those vintage dresses, and how, although it was probably the most toned part of my body, it was not altogether flat; it had a gentle layer of baby fat as some yogurts have a silken layer of cream on top.

For me, the experience of wearing vintage dresses was a sexual education of sorts—a heightening of my awareness of my own flesh, long before any man ever actually touched me, beyond the lightest and most courtly of good-night kisses. Putting on that first pink cocktail dress felt sexual as no other article of clothing ever had to me. So did all the other dresses I bought after it: the summertime picnic ones and tennis ones and prim-wool winter-office ones, and the Lolita playsuits and painterly patterned circle skirts and bullet-breasted halter tops. It turned out that for this type of clothing I had the perfect figure—the petite hourglass. Never once in the whole time I wore vintage did I have to take anything to the tailor for alterations, only repairs. I was much fussed over by the owners of certain vintage stores because I could fit into the most outlandishly curved of the 1950s dresses, the ones that were too small in the waist and too full in the bust for most customers to fit into. Fitting into these dresses, that was the ceremony, that was the grand event: the zipping-in often felt more sexual than actually wearing them out in public. I loved the sucking in, the sweet wishy breathlessness; how rusty side-zippers snaked along creamy skin—one wrong swerve and their teeth might nibble my flesh!—and how then in one swift motion they fastened into place.

Sometimes it seemed to me that these dresses—these

same cotton dresses that could look so heartbreakingly innocent crossing the lawn on a summer's evening, that harkened back to the era of sock hops and glass-bottled Coca-Colas and sherbet-colored Cadillacs—had been designed with a naughty streak in mind. A pair of robin's-egg blue bloomers peeked out from beneath the gingham kick pleats of one of my tennis dresses (*not* that I ever played tennis). Turn over a rickrack hem and find a threaded ribbon of red lace below. One of the sundresses, also gingham, had little silver snaps located on the insides of the shoulder straps; pull the snaps apart and the dress fell open to the breasts. Sometimes beneath the skirt of a dark tweed dress there would be gnashes in the slippery silk of the lining: a suggestion of ravishment.

"Can you fit a meal inside of that?" the waiters said, scanning my figure when I entered the dining room, adding, "*That* is some waist."

During these years, I went to an artsy, progressive private school in the suburbs, where my whimsical style was probably an asset and I did, for the first time in my life, have a number of friends my own age. But I was still "the girl whose mother owns the Pudding," and the restaurant continued to be the main setting of my social life; it was my clubhouse, as it were, my private world to which I allowed other people tantalizing glimpses.

On school nights, to break up the tedium of homework and commuting and New England winters, my friends and I used to do "dress-up" dinners. Our favorite things to order were red meat and chocolate, although these days, when I meet old friends for lunch in some East Coast city or other, we all seem to order the same beet salads with prickly greens and thin dressings, and it isn't the same; nothing is the same. But then we all wore vintage dresses, we piled our wrists with bangles and our necks with pop-bead pearls, and drank "Bondage Shirley Temples" trailing lime and lemon peels. We flirted with waiters, gay and straight, though it seems to me now that the gay ones always excited our imaginations more than the straight ones. I don't think it was just because they were more handsome—although I suppose that some of them must have been—but because we understood from all the old movies we had ever seen and all the novels we had ever read that unrequited love was sexiest.

There was one colorful young man I had something of a crush on in those years. His name was Drew.

He was such a dandy that he once told my mother, "I'll quit if you don't write bow tie privileges into my contract."

The Pudding, alas, had a dress code for the staff now. It wasn't like the old days, when the waitresses wore different white blouses and the waiters wore jewel-toned cummerbunds. Now both waiters and waitresses wore black pants and starched white shirts issued from our linen supplier, with black shoes that the managers were supposed to check for scuffs and holes. But Drew—and I admired him for this—would have none of it. He told me that he suspected that our latest general manager, himself a flamboyant dresser, had made up the dress code because he feared competition from the staff. When Drew told my mother that he suffered from a shortage of closet space and had had to put portable clothing racks in his bedroom, as she herself had, she made an exception in his case. Anyone who loved clothes as much as she did didn't need to follow the dress code.

Drew had a shaved head. "Imagine," my mother said, "how high maintenance it would be to keep up that shaved head. *I* can barely keep up my highlights."

Some of the line cooks had shaved heads, too, but Drew's was different. No one had ever seen a speck of hair on it, and the skin looked as pristine as the shell of a peppermint candy. Drew drank three brandy snifters full of whole milk a day. He carried an old-fashioned doctor's bag full of packages of vanilla wafers with him at all times. His collection of bow ties rivaled my mother's collection of high heels in quantity, and they were very beautiful: I remember in particular a rich blue velvet one. He also wore top hats, which he propped on the oversized bottles of champagne behind the bar. Sometimes I didn't notice the top hats, because they fit in with the rest of the antiquated clutter in the dining room. As Drew himself said, "I *go* with this restaurant."

Drew's appearance won him presents as well as attention. At the Bastille Day festival on Holyoke Street—a sweaty affair in which the Pudding, along with other restaurants in the Square, was forced to set up a booth and sell beignets and sausages to tourists—he got free sticks of cotton candy because they went so well with his straw hat and seersucker suit. One of the waitresses, who also worked as a first grade teacher, had her students scamper around the classroom, collecting feathers and rhinestones so they could make Drew an Easter bonnet to wear at brunch.

But it was Mariness Dewitt III, one of our regular customers, who gave the most extravagant gift. Every year, Mariness celebrated his birthday alone on the terrace with a glass of sherry and a slice of coconut cake, and every year he would stand up to blow out the candles while the other customers applauded. One afternoon he dropped off a beribboned package for "that delightful bartender." It was an antique top hat, heavy with smoke blue plumes and reeking of moths. "I do want to wear it," Drew said, "but I couldn't feel . . . clean."

Whenever Drew worked, I ate dinner at the bar and felt like a little girl again, even though by now I was a teenager. He gave me some of his vanilla wafers—a treat, because I ate at the Pudding so much, I sometimes got bored of all the desserts on the menu—and milk mixed with ice cubes in a sterling-silver cocktail shaker so that it tasted like the frostiest, purest milk in the world.

*I*t was hot the summer I was seventeen. On the terrace, little old ladies broiled in the sun, clutching Bloody Marys in their wrinkled hands. Whenever I ate outside, I heard the chefs cursing and grunting through the screen of the kitchen. I heard the hiss of the dishwasher and smelled, along with the roses and honeysuckle, bacon frying and blueberries bubbling on the stove in a pot of sugar. Inside, I shed golden hairs on the backs of the red velvet chairs. One afternoon, during lunch, we went through every martini glass in the restaurant—the dishwasher could not scrub them fast enough to keep up with the demand—and for several nights in a row the expediter peeled down to only his boxers in the middle of the line, because he could no longer bear the heat.

Now that I was a teenager, summertime meant boys, the college boys who waited tables in the summer. They came to work in pale Oxford shirts and flip-flops, and stood barechested in the beating sun as they arranged umbrellas and lifted crates of San Pellegrino on the terrace. I could see their muscles, the waistbands of their blue gingham boxers below their tanned midriffs. They smoothed napkins on my lap, brought me thick wedges of coconut cake and slices of grapefruit on ice, and hugged me, at the end of the night, too long and too hard. "The cabana boys," I called them. "My cabana boys."

That summer, I kissed one of the cabana boys. I kissed him nearly every afternoon on the fire escape off the terrace all summer long. He had broad shoulders and put lemon-scented gel in his blond hair, but I liked the back of his neck the best: the line of clean-clipped blond against the tanned flesh. I traced it, softly, with my fingertips.

Some afternoons it was too hot to eat. Then the ice cubes in the mint juleps the cabana boy made me melted before I could take my first sip and the strawberry ices dissolved to pink puddles. Those days, he brought me finger bowls: violets and nasturtiums bobbing in soapy water. He rubbed lily of the valley talcum powder onto my shoulders, and the flecks fell through the cracks in the fire escape and landed like snowflakes on the sizzling red bricks of the sidewalks below. Afterward, he pressed his lips to my shoulder and smeared the powder, like powdered sugar on a petit four after you take your first bite.

When he went to check on his tables, I lay back on the fire escape, the rails digging through my cotton dresses, my head throbbing from booze. I gazed at the slate roofs against the blue sky and waited for him to return.

He vanished, of course, at the end of the summer; all the cabana boys did. Out of everyone in the restaurant business, only they kept a reliable schedule.

But I dreamed about those boys, the cabana boys, and wondered if they ever dreamed about me after they had gone. Once, late at night in an ice-cream parlor, I ran into the blond one; he had a girl on his arm. As I stood there under the fluorescent lights, I realized just what an enchanted environment the Pudding could be. In the real world, it was unlikely that many of these cabana boys ever would have given me a second look. But at the Pudding, what had worked in my favor? Did they want to break the rules and flirt with the boss's daughter? Or was it something else— something drowsy and sensual in the air on those empty summer afternoons, the red velvet chairs baking in the thick golden light? In any case, I attributed their attraction to me to the romance of the atmosphere, and not to any budding sexuality of my own.

Just before I left for college my mother had an unfortunate incident with a representative from Harvard Real Estate.

Now that the restaurant was getting so busy, there was too much garbage to fit into the Dumpsters in the alley at the end of the night. This looked untidy, and it attracted rats as well, which already menaced that parking lot. Harvard Real Estate complained to my mother, insisting that she find a way to reduce the amount of garbage.

In the old days, the dishwashers used to hurl the bags of garbage off of the fire escape, aiming for the Dumpster. In most cases, they landed there. But one night, a bag fell on the roof of the car of a representative from Harvard Real Estate just as he was stepping into the parking lot. Some people might have had a sense of humor about this (*we* did), but not this man. He was livid, and stormed back into the building, where after much commotion he found my mother and demanded that she pick up the spilled garbage herself. It was raining that day and there were scraps of wilted produce in the mud at the foot of the Dumpster. I saw my mother kneeling on the ground and holding a radish peel in her hands. The man from Harvard Real Estate, in a sleekly tailored navy suit, was standing over her and watching.

At the time, though, my mother was dating a man with a caustic sense of humor and a feisty temper. Word of the incident in the parking lot got round to him, and the next time he saw this man in the building, at the foot of the staircase outside the Members' Lounge, he looked him straight in the eye and called him "a miserable little prick." The man demanded an apology letter. My mother's boyfriend did just that, adding, "And I think I did a damn fine job." When I asked why, he said that he referenced the encounter at the foot of the stairs as many times as he could, making sure to include the phrase "miserable little prick" a number of times in the letter.

In the end, staff memos went up all over the restaurant. They read: DO NOT THROW ANYTHING OFF THE FIRE ESCAPE! THIS IS GROUNDS FOR IMMEDIATE DISMISSAL. Whenever I saw one, I got a faint little chill, a premonition of forces beyond my control, or even, more alarmingly, beyond my mother's.

At the time of the incident with the man in the alley, I didn't feel anger on my mother's behalf. That came later, when I myself was a grown woman. Then, what I felt was fear. I wanted to appease the man from Harvard Real Estate more than I wanted to rescue my mother. As I saw it, the main thing to be rescued in the situation was not a person, but a place: the Pudding, without which, I knew, the pink lights would be extinguished, and the magic erased for everyone.

Fourteen

THE LAST
OF THE SHIRLEY
TEMPLES

I left for college in the fall of 1999, and returned home for Thanksgiving break to find everyone at the Pudding in the midst of elaborate preparations for what promised to be the giddiest holiday season ever. *The Boston Globe* wrote of my mother's New Year's menu: "Splendidly dressed up for a Victorian Christmas, the Pudding's dining room is a classic setting for a refined New Year's. Four- and five-course menus will be served amid the soft sounds of the Dan Fox Trio. Each table will be set with a traditional croquembouche, a grand French cream puff dessert, to be devoured with the finale of chocolate fondue. Homemade gold-leafed fortune cookies, gifts, and dancing await guests of the second seating."

We rang in the year 2000 in the dining room at the Pudding, under the swaying canopy of pink tissue-paper stars. Champagne glasses were raised in toasts, fortune cookies opened, fortunes read aloud. The cream puffs, laced with curlicues of dripping dark chocolate, sat in the middle of the table.

That night, I wore a strapless lilac tulle dress. Later on, I would wear that same dress under very different circumstances.

Meanwhile, against this backdrop of fin de siècle decadence, the Hasty Pudding Club was going to seed. The finances of the Club had never been all that stable since the early eighties, when changing times had forced them to shut the private dining room and rent the third floor space to the restaurant. And more recently, we would later learn, two of its members had been embezzling money from the Club's bank account, using it to finance extravagant shopping excursions, parties, and trips. The students eventually pleaded guilty to larceny in 2002.

When the Club finally declared bankruptcy, it put the restaurant in exactly the powerless position we had always feared. My mother and Mary-Catherine filed a lawsuit against Harvard Real Estate, trying to build a case to extend our lease. Things got contentious. An item appeared in the *Globe* in which someone from Harvard Real Estate criticized us for occasionally bouncing our rent checks and hosting luncheons for the Hasty Pudding members instead of paying our bills.

In October 2000, Harvard Real Estate ended months

of discussion by reaching an agreement with the Club: it would pay off their debts in exchange for acquiring the building. It also agreed to take on the cost—then estimated at ten million dollars—of the repairs and rewiring necessary to improve the state of the building.

That November, my mother and Mary-Catherine lost their lawsuit. Harvard and the restaurant reached a compromise in which legal lawsuits would be dropped and the restaurant would serve patrons until Commencement 2001 had passed.

My mother broke the news to me over the phone, when I was home from college, on the morning of Thanksgiving. It was a holiday and, as always in the restaurant business, the show had to go on. They were expecting more than four hundred customers later that day.

"Do you have a second?" she asked.

Being home on break, I had slept late. I was standing in our kitchen rubbing sleep from my eyes when she said, "I wanted to let you know because it's going to be in the paper and I don't want you to find out that way. Are you listening?"

In the background, I heard the usual sounds of chaos that accompanied my mother when she was at the restaurant— the sounds of the kitchen.

"Uh-huh."

"Cardamom panna cotta!" my mother was saying. "Cardamom panna cotta, Charlotte? Would you believe that's what these new young pastry chefs think people want to eat on Thanksgiving? People want pecan pie! Baked apples! Charlotte au chocolat!" She laughed. "Well, anyway. I just wanted to let you know that things didn't go so well with Harvard. Wouldn't you know? We lost the lease."

My mother paused, then went on. "We don't have to close right away. Not till June, not till after graduation. June sixteenth—that's a Saturday—that will be the last night of business." She paused again, and when I didn't say anything, kept talking. "I don't have a lot of time to spend talking about this now—for God's sake, it's Thanksgiving—but promise me something. Promise you won't cry in the dining room tonight, or anything like that. Oh, that reminds me, what are you going to wear tonight? That green velvet with the low back? I loved that one . . . Oh! Gotta go! Expecting four hundred of our nearest and dearest."

The next morning, I went into the restaurant to help decorate the Christmas tree for the last time. I felt that this was an important ritual for me to take part in. When I entered the dining room, in the white angora sweater and red velveteen skirt I had chosen for the occasion, I saw that my mother, already standing on the ladder, had left her fur-trimmed holiday mules at home. There were already sprigs of holly in her hair.

"It's a good thing you came," she said. "We've got to get the tree up before lunch. I need all the help I can get."

Decorating had begun. My mother already had draped her bead collection over several four-tops in the corner. But it was the pile of cardboard boxes marked *Ornaments* in front of the waiters' station that interested me. I had shown up to see and to treasure for the last time our old ornaments, the ones members of the staff had made for the Christmas parties. Come the move in June, I expected no one would remember to keep the ornaments. When I opened the first box, dust wafted onto my white sweater, and I coughed. Inside, wrapped in tissue paper, I saw the pink glass bulbs and dangling hearts my mother had bought in bulk at Saks Fifth Avenue. The next two boxes revealed the same. In the fourth box, my mother had packed more ropes of beads. I found wads of tissue paper and shards of violet glass in the last box, but none of the old ornaments: the expired Neiman Marcus charge card trimmed in red glitter, the model of the Pudding staircase, the silver-painted rib.

"Where are all the other ornaments?" I asked. "The ones from the Christmas parties?"

"Charlotte, I don't know," she said, staring down at me from the ladder. "They're *somewhere*. Hang this mistletoe, will you?"

I stood there, biting my nails.

"Listen," she said, "what does it matter? We still have all our Christmas ornaments at home."

We had not used our Christmas ornaments at home since we had lost the farmhouse. That was thirteen years ago now. What did *those* ornaments matter?

While my mother was in a flurry of activity decorating the tree, I walked out of the dining room and lay down on the sofa on the second-floor landing, where I hadn't taken a nap in years. One Saturday night, I remembered, an old lady in a black dress and pearls had kicked off her spectator pumps and slept there during the eight o'clock rush. When one of the managers had roused her, fearing she had passed out, she had said, "Oh, no! It's just such a *marvelous* sofa." It *was* a marvelous sofa: wine-colored in some lights and fudge-colored in others, with deep cushions, big enough for a dozen little girls to have squeezed onto at my birthday parties. The leather had held up beautifully over the past century. Yet the sofa was, of course, old; old like the bottles of Scotch in our investors' liquor cabinets, old like the cashmere sweaters their wives slung over their shoulders on lunch dates, old like their whitewashed beach houses on the Cape. It was old, I realized, like Harvard.

Now, lying by myself on the sofa, I realized that just when I most wanted to despise Harvard for no longer having room for us, I couldn't. I had grown up in this world as no one else had, and if the clunky antiquity of Strawberry Night and the Krokodiloes revealed something about the world itself, it also revealed something about *me*. It had defined my tastes and my sensibilities and, no doubt, my sense of alienation from members of my own generation—a condition which even the experience of leaving home and going to college had not yet broken.

In my childhood, in which we had changed addresses so many times, 10 Holyoke Street had been my only home; I had even used it as my address. Now, with the news of the lease ending, I could no longer delude myself that it had ever been mine at all. We were only renters. It had never really been ours.

That February, I went back to college for the spring semester of my sophomore year, and I turned twenty years old. And that May, I came back to my dorm room to discover that the light on my phone was blinking. I had a message from my mother in which she said to call her back immediately. I called, only to learn that my father had had a heart attack and was now recovering in the hospital.

"Would you believe it," she said, "it happened right *in the middle of the investor dinner*! That *would* happen to me, the way my life is going. Who am I kidding? It's the way my life has always been. You know these rich people who are always going on safari? Not me! I don't have to go looking for adventure; I get plenty of it in the restaurant business. Well, anyway, the doctor I talked to said he's doing okay, all things considered. He did say that he'd better give up smoking . . . Let me give you the number at the hospital. You can call him if you want."

During the time since I went away to college, my father, never a dominant figure in our lives, had been drifting away from us and deeper and deeper into the kind of defiant bohemianism that had long since fallen out of fashion in the modern world, seeking, as his hero John Cage once said, "to make poverty elegant." His most recent madcap scheme was enrolling as a student at the Museum School, because he'd noticed that if you were a student, you got your own studio for free. So my father, with works in the permanent collections of the Museum of Fine Arts, Boston, and the Guggenheim, got a full scholarship to the Museum School as an undergraduate, for he himself, like so many bright, embattled people of his generation, had dropped out of college in the sixties.

I myself was a student at Bennington, where, I had discovered, one could count on hearing the name "John Cage" with some frequency. I often observed the black-clad music students playing his pieces in the romantically run-down, gray stone music building, and I had attended several senior concerts based on his work. But Bennington was, notoriously, a rich kids' school, and I was on scholarship. To me, no poverty was elegant, and least of all my father's.

But he was in the hospital. He had almost died. I pictured him, wheezing, with the paper sheets pulled up to his chin. I wondered where he would go afterward to recuperate. I realized that I didn't even know where he was living at this point.

I got off the phone with my mother and called the number of the hospital where he was recovering. A receptionist transferred me to his extension, where a nurse picked up the phone. I asked if I could speak to Michael Silver.

"Well, that depends. Are you a relative or a friend or what?"

I said I was his daughter.

"Oh," she said. "Well, sure, you can talk to him. I didn't know he had a daughter."

My father, on the other line, was laughing—faint, croaking laughs. He had some friends visiting him.

"You know, Char, the food's okay in here," he said. "As good as some of the yuppie catering joints I've worked at, let me tell you. I'm loving the lime Jell-O! Thinking of photographing it one of these days. Though I always send back the cottage cheese. Can't fucking stand that stuff."

Then he asked about me, and I mumbled something about the Pudding closing. June sixteenth would be the last night of business, I said.

"Oh, I heard about that," said my father, coughing. And then, as I had heard him say with the utmost conviction so many times before, "God, am I ever glad I got out of the restaurant business."

One afternoon that June, a few days before the Pudding closed, a postcard caught my eye while I was browsing in Harvard Book Store. The postcard showed a photograph of the center of the Square, between Out of Town News and The Tasty, before The Tasty had closed. It was winter, and it had just snowed. The photographer must have taken the picture late at night, because no footprints had trampled the snow and Harvard Square looked, under the streetlamps, serene.

In the blistering sunshine outside, Harvard Square looked different than I remembered. The Abercrombie & Fitch loomed over the sidewalks like a shining Buick in a lot of crumbling roadsters; the Hawaiian shirts in the window of Pacific Sunwear looked as bright as a handful of Skittles; white letters stamped the red sign of the brand-new Staples. I had rested, only moments earlier, on a stoop in the Pit (the punks had vanished and the graffiti had faded) and read the words frosted on the Abercrombie window: SUMMER 2001. SUN YOUR BUNS. HIT THE SURF. FLIRT LIKE CRAZY.

I stared at the postcard; I had been there, once. Sometimes, on winter nights, when the snow had drifted past the fire escapes and the kitchen smelled of brioche and the bar of hot toddies, my mother and I had locked the restaurant after everyone else had gone and stepped outside into the snowbanks. In all of Harvard Square, no one was awake but the two of us. The snowflakes floated down, starred her collar lush with feathers, fizzled on my Mary Janes. We held hands, my mother and I; we walked down the street together.

The day before the last day, I bought two dozen pink balloons, on trade, from Serge the florist and brought them to the Pudding. I had thought we could snip the tassels, my mother and I, and hold hands as the balloons fluttered up to the vaulted ceiling and blurred with the tissue paper stars. But once she saw them, my mother suggested cutting them loose on the terrace instead.

"You take them outside," she said. "I'll be back in a second."

Then she scrambled back to the kitchen, and I stepped onto the terrace. The terrace looked like a pink and brown garden now; the flowers had all started to wilt.

"Here we go!" she said, click-clacking across the floor. "If this can cut through the cowboy steak, it can cut through some balloons."

The butcher knife in her hands glinted in the sunlight, and for a brief moment I looked at my mother's hands. Calluses bulged in the centers of her palms and one of her garish pink nails had split in half; she badly needed a manicure, but by now, I suppose, she didn't care. Then, before I could say a word, she hacked the strings in half and two dozen pink balloons bobbed above Harvard Square. They soared above the slate roofs and then were gone.

P osture is everything.
        Or so my mother was forever telling me. I tried to remember this advice on the last night of the Pudding, June 16, 2001. Shoulders back, head held high, I walked up, up the white-painted staircase toward the third floor.

I opened the heavy black doors to the dining room.

Lashes blackened, hair combed and fluffed, I wore a highly stylized, romantic dress out of a Degas painting, a strapless tea-length in lilac tulle. Beneath the skirt there were fragile tinted crinolines, one rose, one green, one pale gold. With this dress I wore a pair of gold kid slippers.

The dining room was full of customers; hardly any tables were empty. This beautiful June night, seats outside on the herb-garden terrace were especially coveted. Conversation spilled through the wide-open French doors. Waiters were carrying martinis on silver trays covered with pink linen napkins. The night air was fragrant with lavender, with thyme. The customers would toast to the last night of the Pudding amidst the ruins of terra-cotta urns and nasturtium vines.

It was only then, imagining the customers outside making toasts to the last night of the Pudding, that I realized that the loss of the Pudding was not only a personal event but a public one. I thought of how whenever a business closed that you used to go to, you missed it, as my father spoke of missing the pastrami sandwiches at Elsie's, my mother the butterscotch sundaes at Bailey's, after they closed. I thought, of course, of the passing of The Tasty, and of how, after Savenor's burned down when I was eleven, my Friday nights with my father were never the same without their roast-beef sandwiches. When a business closed, it meant that no new memories could be made there. So now, come next June, there would still be icy, bracing martinis somewhere in the world, but not on this roof deck, not like this, not here. There would be no place to get my mother's lobster salad with nasturtium blossoms, no way to quench a thirsting for her gazpacho with chive oil and rock shrimp. Such things were the tiny, jewel-like neighborhood rituals that bit by bit compose a world, a life. And by living on in memory, they composed the inner life, too, which maybe, in the end, was the only thing that mattered.

At the threshold of the dining room, various people approached and hugged me. They blew air kisses and exclaimed, "Charlotte! Such a beautiful dress!" Some of these people I recognized, and some of them I didn't. But I pretended I recognized them all. I composed myself, saying, in my best front-room voice, "Hello, hello."

And somewhere, somewhere across the dining room, my mother also was standing straight and saying, "Hello, hello." People would believe that she meant it; people would be enfolded in the scent of her Joy perfume, her cleavage a bed of jasmine and roses. "Hello, hello . . ."

And then, I saw her. She was standing in front of the bar, in conversation, in transit. The silver beads frosting her Tiffany blue cashmere sweater caught the light from the chandeliers. She looked soft, my mother.

She did not see me.

I continued to stand in the dining room, taking it all in. Then Mary-Catherine brushed past me, rolling her eyes and saying, "What a night! Would you believe it?" Then she named another restauranteur in the Square and said, "They actually sent their lamb back. Now, you know me, ordinarily I'm Miss Hospitality, I say the customer is always right. But you think people could have a little respect on the last night! Your mother is furious. She says, when to think *our* closing is only going to help *their* business—"

But then somebody came up to Mary-Catherine and hugged her, too, and now there she was, saying, "Hello, hello . . ."

I sat down at A-1. I waited, and as I did, I realized that the experience was reminiscent of how I used to wait for my mother at the end of the night when I was a child. Only it didn't quite feel like nighttime yet, because by now it was the middle of June, and we were coming up on the longest day of the year. The dining room looked, on evenings like this, quite beautiful, its high, beamed ceilings filled with angelic light. The gold threads in the green velvet carpet shimmered and looked, almost, hot to the touch.

All around me, I saw waiters bearing dishes, pink-lit lobsters and lambs, mauve-skinned new potatoes and fat, blushing cranberry beans.

I read the menu. But somehow, nothing quite appealed. What I wanted were all of the things that weren't on the menu anymore and hadn't been in years: the things my father used to make. There was one dish, in particular, I craved. It was an appetizer from the early days of the Pudding: smoked pheasant and Roquefort flan. And then it occurred to me that I didn't even want smoked pheasant and Roquefort flan plated and served as a proper appetizer, but rather, I wanted to eat a pheasant leg, cold, the way I sometimes used to hanging out in the kitchen on hazy summer nights just like this one. Certain foods were best savored like that—all by themselves, without fixings. You could get straight to the purity of their flavors then. My father could have told you that. It was Carla, the old line cook, who used to twist off the dimpled, fatty pheasant legs just for me. But Carla, like so many people who used to work at the Pudding, was gone, and I had no idea whatever had become of her.

I waited and waited, and no one came over to the table to take my order. So, conscious that I was alone and worried that I had nothing to do with my hands, I read the menu again. Of course I understood that the waiters were busy; no doubt the kitchen was in the weeds, too, and even if I got to order, it would take forever for the food to come. It was going to be what my mother called "one of those nights," which meant off-kilter, awry, no accounting for delays and disasters.

Some time passed, and a waiter came over to my table. I immediately saw that he was out of breath and had no time to talk to me.

"Oh, hey, Charlotte," he said. "Crazy night tonight. But what can I get you to drink?"

"May I please have a Shirley Temple?"

I hadn't drunk Shirley Temples in years. I was twenty years old, and they had not been my signature beverage for quite some time. But tonight, I was convinced that no other beverage would do. I recalled brandy snifters thick with grenadine, bunches of maraschino cherries queasy-sweet and dripping with dye, that one cool, saving pinch of ginger ale.

As I waited for the waiter to come back with my Shirley Temple, I heard a peal of laughter ring across the dining room. It was my mother's laughter; it was unmistakable. And then I knew. She would never sit down. Never.

The waiter came back with my beverage and placed it in front of me.

"Here you go," he said. "Enjoy."

The bartender had served my Shirley Temple—my last Shirley Temple—in a tall, plain glass. The liquid was a tepid red, almost blush, and a lone maraschino cherry bobbed at the top like a bloated goldfish. It looked like the Shirley Temples at other restaurants—a beverage for a stranger. But I drank it, and heard the hollow rasp of the straw sapping the ice cubes dry; they drained from pink to gray and finally crusted the bottom of the glass like splintered rhinestones.

Oh, I had wanted to remember everything. But I couldn't do it; I didn't have the strength for this particular good-bye. All of a sudden, I started to feel faint. The dining room blurred before me, the grassy carpet rolling and the rose-colored lightbulbs melting. Tears welled in my eyes. Soon they would plop onto the tablecloth, and everyone would see. "No crying at the restaurant, Charlotte," my mother had told me when I was a little girl. "Remember, it's a public place."

I got up from the table. I went down one flight to the ladies' room, locking myself in the same stall where, earlier that evening, I'd put on the lilac tulle dress and done my makeup. Now I was crying and my mascara was running. I grabbed a tissue and tried to mop up the streaks. Maybe I could pull myself together and go back upstairs and sit down to dinner again. Maybe—

I was standing at the sink, washing my face, when the door to the ladies' room swung open and I heard stilettos striking the tiles. They made a cold sound; they pinged, like ice cubes falling in a glass. I straightened my shoulders, ready for the inevitable confrontation.

"Charlotte."

My mother's voice was strident now, nothing soft, nothing lambent about it. There in the ladies' room we were offstage and we didn't have to pretend. This was the unyielding voice, the voice of the kitchen and not the front room, the voice that had earned her the name "Patton in Pumps."

"Charlotte, I heard that you left the dining room in tears. God knows I shouldn't have to be dealing with this tonight, but here I am."

I burst into tears all over again.

"Charlotte. Open the door."

I opened the door. My mother stormed into the stall, bolting the door shut behind her. Her teardrop rhinestone earrings glittered in the savage white fluorescent light of the ladies' room, so different from the light we were used to in the dining room, where everything was rose and gold, enchanted and indirect.

"For God's sake. It's my restaurant and it's going out of business. And tomorrow, tomorrow I'm the one who has to figure out the rest of my life. Do you see me crying? Do you? Do you? Have you ever seen me crying? Have you? Do you see Mary-Catherine crying? There's no crying in the dining room."

My mother had taken her sunglasses off, and I could see, so close to mine, her face, as stylized after its own fashion as a Kabuki mask: the lustrous violet lips, sea-foam powder applied at mysterious, softening angles around her eyes, and the doll-like contrast of arched black eyebrows and teased blond hair. She had put on this face while her stage set—her restaurant—was crumbling right in front of her.

It took me years, years after that night, to understand her

attitude. And, later, to even admire it. The style; the verve; the queenly exit strategy; nothing apologetic, nothing wistful, nothing *weak*, about it. Yes, I would leave, I would lose the Pudding, I would grow up. I would know other losses, other defeats, and I would come to realize that my mother's behavior was quite splendid.

I never saw the dining room again. I knew that sitting down to dinner, as though nothing had happened, was out of the question. I had shattered the spell and was cast out from the kingdom.

So with a sweep of black taffeta my mother went back to her court, and I dried my eyes. I left the ladies' room. I walked slowly down the stairs. I felt the weight of my mother's words and I composed myself; I did not scamper, did not run. At the foot of the staircase, one torn gold ribbon sagged off the banister. After I walked through the heavy black double doors to the building, I heard the *thud* when they slammed shut behind me.

Outside, darkness had fallen. I hailed a taxi by the corner of Out of Town News. It was only then, climbing into the car and feeling my bare shoulders stick to the ridged leather seat, that I remembered I had not eaten dinner. I would be hungry later.

POSTSCRIPT

*I*f I had it to do all over again, if I could go back there, under the vaulted green ceiling, the rosy tissue-paper stars, I'd sit right back down at the table and I would order, I would taste once more, my mother's famous roasted-sweet-red-pepper soup. I'd even eat my last supper alone; maybe, now, I'd even prefer it that way, honor it as part of the fine tradition of the solitary childhood that made me who I am. Shoulders back, head up, my mother's daughter, I'd have a grand time of it. I'd drain the beautiful red bowl dry. I'd get up from that table and walk out of that dining room and never look back. I'd perfect the art of the sublime good-bye.

When, not too long after the Pudding closed, my mother and Mary-Catherine opened a new restaurant in Harvard Square, customers who still pined for that soup went in asking for it. My mother put it on the menu for a time, but soon it vanished, never to return. She wasn't in the kitchen anymore and didn't trust the new crop of hot young chefs making it. It was too labor-intensive, the new chefs said. It was too rich. It used too many cunning and delicate varieties of peppers, too many guiltless lashings of heavy cream. We live in a new century now and a whole different world. And now, now that I am thinking about it, I blame the failure of that splendid soup in our contemporary moment on something else. I think, probably, those chefs were simply too young to coax out that fatty, candied thickness, the broken flavors, suave and rustic, sensuous and sad—a winter's soup, a woman's soup. I think they didn't know anything, those chefs. I think they hadn't lived. My mother herself was already in her forties and divorced when she came up with the recipe. When I was a young girl, I didn't appreciate it.

Now I do.

ACKNOWLEDGMENTS

Many grateful acknowledgments go to my agent, Emily Forland, and editor, Sarah McGrath; to early readers Edward Hoagland, Dan Hofstadter, Sigrid Nunez, David Semanki, and Kathleen Spivack; to my friends and family; and to all of the wonderful and wacky people who worked at the Pudding over the years, whether my fond memories of you appear in this book or not.